RATTLED

Ellis Gunn is originally from Scotland where she published three poetry collections, one of which was shortlisted for the Saltire First Book of the Year Award. Her work was also anthologised in *Dreamstate: New Scottish Poets* (Polygon), *Ahead Of Its Time* (Jonathan Cape), *Modern Scottish Women Poets* (Canongate) and 100 *Favourite Scottish Poems* (Luath Press).

RATTLED

A rare, first person account of surviving a stalker

ELLIS GUNN

ALLEN&UNWIN

SYDNEY·MELBOURNE·AUCKLAND·LONDON

Allen & Unwin
83 Alexander Street
Crows Nest NSW 2065
Australia
Phone: (61 2) 8425 0100
Email: info@allenandunwin.com
Web: www.allenandunwin.com

 A catalogue record for this book is available from the National Library of Australia

ISBN 978 1 76106 599 6

Set in 12/18.5 pt Sabon by Midland Typesetters, Australia
Printed and bound in Australia by Griffin Press

10 9 8 7 6 5 4 3 2 1

The paper in this book is FSC® certified. FSC® promotes environmentally responsible, socially beneficial and economically viable management of the world's forests.

Contents

Why this book

There are so many reasons not to write this book. In writing this, I'm putting myself in danger. In writing this, I'm revealing things about myself I'd rather nobody knew, to anyone who cares to listen.

I've questioned my motives and my sanity a hundred times. What is it *for*, this book? Why am I putting myself through it? I'd like to say it's all about wanting to help others, but it's more selfish than that. Maybe it's partly about sharing experiences and making connections that resonate with the world, but I think it's mostly a desire to come to some kind of peace with those experiences, to understand them more fully. 'We are collectors not of memories so much as those memories' shadows so that we might recover, through their nurturing darkness, the hidden meaning of our lives,' says Philip Graham.[1] 'The task of a memoirist is not only to reveal the shadow in isolation but to find the hidden, larger structure.' Thoreau, famously quoted by Annie Dillard, puts it another way; 'Know your own bone: gnaw at it, bury it, unearth it, and gnaw it still.'[2] While I was writing this book, my own bone often terrified me, but I couldn't leave it alone.

I was constantly drawn back to the dark soil it was buried in, scrabbling in the earth until I had it, once again, between my teeth.

At my lowest point, when fear slopped around in the bowl of my stomach and I came closest to abandoning the book and leaving the bone buried safely out of sight, I came across the old English folktale 'Mr Fox'.[3]

It's the story of a young woman, Lady Mary, who has 'two brothers and more lovers than she can count'. Her favourite lover is the gallant Mr Fox, and eventually the two decide to get married. Mary asks Mr Fox where they will live, and he describes his enormous castle and where it is, but for some mysterious reason he won't take her to see it.

Mary decides to go look for herself, and after traipsing across the countryside for yumpty-tum days—lo and behold, the castle in all its glory, just as Mr Fox described it. Its walls are high, its moat is deep, but above the gate is a most peculiar motto:

Be Bold, Be Bold.

Well, says Mary to herself, *I AM pretty bold,* and she strides through the open gate and on to the door of the castle. Over this door is a longer version of the first motto:

Be Bold, Be Bold, But Not Too Bold.

Come on now, says Mary, *make up your mind,* but she carries on into the hall and up the main staircase. On the first floor she finds another door, above which is a third version of the motto:

Be Bold, Be Bold, But Not Too Bold,
Lest That Your Heart's Blood Should Run Cold.

Undeterred, and determined to find out what is going on, Mary flings open the door of the chamber. Right in front of her is a disgusting, mishmashed pile of rotting corpses and yellow-boned skeletons. Somehow Lady Mary can tell that these were once the bodies of beautiful young women. If she doesn't want to end up in the stinking pile, she needs to get her own beautiful body out of there.

She clip-clops down the stairs and through the hall, but uh-oh, who's this tramping across the courtyard, dragging a young woman's body behind him? It's only her erstwhile lover, Mr Fox!

Lady Mary quickly hides behind a wine cask that Fox has left at the foot of the stairs. She watches as he yanks the body across the floor, but just as he reaches the staircase, he stops. A diamond ring, glittering on the finger of the young woman, has caught his eye. He tries to pull it off, but he can't shift it, so he wheechs out his sword and chops the poor woman's hand off. A bit too enthusiastically, as it turns out, because the hand flies through the air and lands in the lap of Lady Mary, still crouched behind the cask. Mr Fox has a quick glance around, but when he can't find the hand he shrugs his shoulders and hauls the body, bumpity-bump, up the stairs to his Chamber of Horrors.

Mary doesn't hang about. She hotfoots it out of there, the lifeless hand in her pocket.

As it happens, Mary and Mr Fox are to be married the very next day. Fox and the wedding guests arrive and they all sit down to a celebration feast before the contract is signed. Fox remarks that Mary's looking a bit peaky and she explains that she hasn't slept much, due to a bad dream.

How interesting, says Fox, *let's hear it.*

Certainly, says Mary, and she tells the wedding party everything that happened to her in Fox Castle.

Not true, says Mr Fox. *Didn't happen. Fake news.*

But it did happen, says Mary, *and here's the hand to prove it.* She pulls the hand from her pocket and points the festering fingers at Mr Fox.

Lady Mary's brothers and friends leap to their feet, draw their swords and 'cut Mr Fox into a thousand pieces'. Maybe not exactly a thousand—they probably weren't counting—but it's certainly the end of Mr Fox, and the end of the story, too.

———

What I loved about this tale was Mary. Unlike the heroines of the fairy tales I had grown up with (Cinderella, Sleeping Beauty, Snow White), Mary wasn't a helpless princess, lounging around waiting for a prince to rescue her. She had a whole bunch of lovers but she chose Mr Fox for herself, and when something about him seemed a bit dodgy, she trusted her instincts and went off and did her own investigating. She was bold and brave and curious, and her boldness paid off—she realised just in time that she was about to marry a misogynistic murderer and she quickly rallied some allies who helped her get out of the situation. Admittedly, it was her brothers who did the final chopping, but only because Mary had got them onside by telling them her story and providing them with evidence. They were the foot soldiers in a plan that Mary had orchestrated. *Be bold, be bold*, the story said to me, *and don't keep quiet about abuse.*

————

So, for better or worse, this is my story. Like the old folk-tales, it's ancient. It's something that happened to me, but it's been happening for hundreds of years. It began before my mother was born, before my granny or even my great-granny was born. Once upon a time, that's how the old tales start, right at the beginning. But the beginning of this story is too far away, too mired in history, so I'll start in the middle.

CHAPTER 1

In the middle.
The third time I met
The Man (the park)

I'm walking through a park, on my way home, having just dropped my son off at school. Or not quite 'just'. I've dropped my son off and I've been to the little café near the school where the coffee is good and the windows fold open onto a quiet, leafy street and a woman with two sausage dogs sits reading the morning paper while her dogs wait patiently by her chair. I've sipped my latte and answered emails and redrafted a poem, and then I've gathered my things and walked back past the school, leaf shadows dancing beneath my feet. I've crossed over the busy road, and now, *now*, I'm walking through this park with its vast beds of heavily laden rosebushes and its avenue of cherry-blossom trees, papery petals of rose and cherry drifting like pink snow along the edges of the path.

Someone calls my name.

I turn round and it's a man on a bicycle, wearing black jeans, black jacket, black bike helmet. He's silhouetted like a shadow against the pink backdrop of the rose beds. His bike is also black. As I turn towards him, a rainbow lorikeet shoots up from the cherry blossom, followed by a gang of noisy miners that swoop and dive around the anxious lori, shattering the air with their raucous squawking, pursuing it as it flees across the open grass.

The man cycles towards me. *Hello*, he says. *You're not on your bike today.*

The wind suddenly picks up, whipping my hair across my face. I scrape the strands out of my eyes and glance round the park, but there's no one else here. It's just me and this man. I turn to look back at the street I just walked along, but there's no one there either. There are only the glass-fronted office blocks and the solid sandstone of colonial municipal buildings. In the distance, traffic roars along the busier road, but the street that leads from there to here is quiet.

nothingnothingnothingnothingnothingnothingnothing

Something dark and clotted heaves inside me but I suppress the urge to lean over and vomit onto the flower beds. Instead, I smile back at the man. *No,* I say, *I had to walk today.*

It's true that I would normally be on my bike. Normally, my son and I cycle to school together. I drop him off, go for a coffee, do a bit of writing, then cycle home. Last night, however, my son left his bike at a friend's house, so this morning we walked, a change to the usual routine. Although this man is not a complete stranger, is someone I've met and spoken to on a couple of occasions, it's odd that he would know anything about my usual routine.

He dismounts from his bike. *Are you on your way home?* he asks. Then, without waiting for an answer, *I'll walk with you.*

And so, here we are, walking along the avenue of cherry trees that leads to the other side of the park. The blossoms drift down and catch in my hair. Tiny stones of panic rattle inside my rib cage as we leave the park and cross over the road to a wide, empty suburban street.

It's funny me bumping into you like this, says the man. *I saw you across the park. I recognised your pants.*

I look down at my trousers. I bought them the weekend before last. I haven't seen this man since I bought them, I don't see how he can recognise them as mine. I consider saying, *I'm sorry, I've forgotten something*, and turning round, going back towards the safer, busier road where the everyday traffic is. But I don't say this, I keep going, caught between the horror of walking alongside him and the fear of angering him by turning back. What might he do? Might he come after me, shove me into a doorway? Would anyone hear me if I screamed? I imagine him chasing me along the deserted street and the dark liquid bubbles up in my throat. I keep walking. He asks me questions and tells me things about himself and I answer politely and engage in conversation and I think how, from the outside, we must look like two people who know each other, who are perhaps even friends, strolling along a suburban street, having a perfectly ordinary conversation, not one person who is potentially psychotic and another who is fighting to hold the wild panic inside herself, who is trying very hard not to ruin the chocolate-box prettiness of the Federation houses with their shiny wrought-iron railings, their clipped lawns and neatly pruned bushes, by spraying the whole damn lot of them with thick, dark, blood-coloured vomit, with thin, bitter bile, with fear and anger and horror.

everythingeverythingeverythingeverythingeverything
everything

CHAPTER 2

Back to the beginning. The first time I met The Man (auction house)

I first met The Man in the park at an auction house. I had been reading poetry at an early morning event in the city centre, the 'Big Bike-Ride Brekky', to celebrate the opening of a new cycle route in Adelaide. The place was buzzing. Food trucks serving free breakfast snags and bacon and egg rolls surrounded the square and the air sparked with the static of the lycra-clad, jostling for free carbs and coffee. Queen was being pumped through the speakers (the band, not the monarch):

BicyclebicyclebicycleIWANTTORIDEMYBICYCLE.

There was someone in cargo shorts doing impressive bike stunts, bouncing through rings of fire and up and down steps, handstanding on the handlebars and backflipping off the saddle. There were Tour Down Under celebrities being interviewed on stage. There was video footage of spectacular race crashes. And there was me, reading bike-related poetry to a crowd of uninterested people who were mostly chatting among themselves, probably trying to fathom why the bejeezus someone had invited a poet to a sporting event.

After my public humiliation, I skulked off to the food stalls to try and get some breakfast. I pled my vegetarian case at two or three different stalls before accepting that the only eggs available were from hens that had been ritually tortured in the name of profit. I settled for a coffee, drank it hurriedly, retrieved my bike and sped across town to catch the auction.

I had become quite a regular at the auction house. I liked it there. I knew the different auctioneers and their particular styles of banter, those who rattled through the lots at top speed and those who took a bit more time. I loved wandering among the lots, looking at collections of bone-china dining sets, Chesterfields and chandeliers, rusted farm tools and dust-covered lamps.

This time I had my eye on a large honey-coloured chest of drawers with inlaid mother-of-pearl knobs and bun feet. I stood in front of it, checking the action of the drawers and looking it over for signs of active woodworm while the bidding murmured on behind me.

A middle-aged man, tall and lean in dark jeans and a Ralph Lauren V-neck, also stopped to have a look. *That's a nice piece*, he said.

Yes, I replied. And then, because it seemed impolite to stop there, *I like the handles.*

They're lovely, aren't they? Are you thinking of bidding on it? he asked.

I was a bit wary. I knew that people sometimes submitted pieces for sale, then got friends to attend the auction and bid for the piece to push the price up. He might be trying to gauge my interest, see how far he could go. *Depends on the price*, I said.

Ah, he replied, *you must be a dealer.*

Good heavens, no. Though maybe I should start. I'm here often enough. I ran my hand across the worn patina of the pine chest.

So what brings you here so often, if you're not a dealer? he asked.

I've just moved into a new house and I'm needing some furniture for it, that's all, I said. *Well, I say a new house. Really it's a very old house.*

He laughed. *Me too*, he said. *A fifties villa in Parkside. I moved in last week.*

Ours is fifties too, I said. *But 1850s.*

That IS old, he said. *I gather from the accent you're not from Australia. Scottish, is it?*

That's right.

Been here long?

Four years.

Not that long then. You must have come for the sunshine. He smiled.

Well, it was my partner's work, really, I said. *It was meant to be a two-year adventure but, well, here we still are. With a house.*

You're not planning on going back then?

Probably not, the bairns are all settled here now. It wouldn't be fair to move them again. I'm the only one that really gets homesick.

Yeah, must be hard, he said. *You must miss your family, your friends.*

Aye, I do, I miss all kinds of things. Even the weather, if you can believe that.

Oh, of course, he said. *All that lovely rain. Why wouldn't you?* We both laughed. *I do know what you mean, though. I've only moved from Sydney, but I still miss it.*

We chatted on for a bit, mostly him asking questions, me responding. He told me he was recently divorced, which had triggered the move to South Australia. He asked me what I did for a living and said he thought I looked arty. I told him I wrote poetry but I certainly didn't make a living out of it.

What's your name, if you don't mind me asking? he said. *I'd like to look you up. Will I be able to read anything of yours online?*

Em, maybe, I said. *Not that I'm well known or anything. But there might be something.* I was starting to feel a bit uncomfortable, though I couldn't really put my finger on why. I think the conversation just felt a bit intense for a chance encounter in an auction house. I told him my name anyway. It didn't occur to me to lie about it. What I really wanted to do was walk away, but it felt like that would be too rude, especially as he was talking again.

Look, I'm not trying to find out where you live or anything, he was saying, *but which suburb is it? I'm still learning where places are in Adelaide and I'm wondering if I know it.*

I think that's what unnerved me most: *I'm not trying to find out where you live or anything.* Why would somebody say that?

It's Prospect, I said hesitantly, not really wanting to give him this information but, again, not quick-witted enough to lie about it, too busy trying to work out how I could politely extricate myself.

I turned to look at the screen that showed which lot was currently being auctioned.

I think I need to move closer to the action, I said. *A piece I want to bid on is coming up soon.*

No worries, he said. *See you later.*

I moved down to the front, near the auctioneer's podium. I found a seat on one of the sofas that was up for auction, and I watched as the different lots appeared on the screen and people held up their numbers or raised a hand to bid for them, but I couldn't focus. I was no longer interested in the honey-coloured chest of drawers. I couldn't explain what it was (a turn of phrase? a certain look?), but something had raised my hackles and I just wanted to go.

The Man was standing between me and the door, so I said goodbye as I went past. *Hey*, he said, *can you give me your phone number or email address? Maybe we could meet for a coffee.*

I gaped at him. *I'm sorry, I don't think that would be appropriate*, I mumbled. I hurried outside, unlocked my bike and cycled home, fast.

———

I don't remember thinking too much about the encounter after that, though it was weird enough for me to tell my partner about it. *This guy I've never met before asked me to go for a coffee with him.* I was curious to know if my partner thought it was unusual behaviour. Maybe I was just being paranoid. My partner agreed that it was a wee bit inappropriate, but hardly a big deal. Just a guy being too keen. Nothing to worry about.

I didn't worry. Not until a few days later when I got an email from him.

Hello there Scottish lassie,
I'm not well today, nasty cold, so I've been lying in bed reading about you. I'd love to discuss your writing sometime. It would be nice to have a coffee with you.

Vague sense of anxiety. There was nothing sinister, but the tone of the email was oddly intimate for someone I'd exchanged a few words with at an auction house. I went back over our conversation. Why on earth had I been so friendly? Had I inadvertently given him the wrong impression? I'd told him heaps about myself without even thinking. I'd given him my real name. I had described myself as 'a poet'. How vain and ridiculous. Maybe this was all my own fault for showing off. There were websites with my contact email address—it wasn't difficult to find if you went looking—and yet, who would email someone who had made it clear they didn't want to be contacted? Who would ask someone to go for a coffee when they'd already said no? I was caught between irritation with myself at being so open and naïve, and irritation with this man for being so persistent, for not taking the hint. I didn't know whether I should reply, telling him to back off, or just ignore the email.

I decided to ignore it. It seemed the politest way of letting him know I wasn't interested. I should have guessed politeness was not going to work with this man.

At school

As a child in Scotland, I am eager to learn. I am words and words and words, I am how and I am why and I am open-eyed and ready. At home my mum reads to me and I want to know how those black marks form themselves into sound. I make my own runes—dashes and curls—pouring out stories that I read back to my dolls. My mum shows me the shapes that make my name and I draw them over and over until I get them right, until they say *this is you*.

On the first day of school my mum and I are early, waiting outside the closed gates. They're opened by a janitor with an iron circle of keys and a brown important coat over his clothes. He holds up a flat palm to show my mum and me that we're not to cross over until he pulls the gates back and fixes them with a metal hook.

My new shoes are Clark's Start-Rite and I look down at their shiny toes as my feet move from the pavement into the playground.

There are two playgrounds, one for boys and one for girls. There's a stone wall with an iron railing between the playgrounds. The railings go up above my head and they have spikes like arrows on top of them. The arrows point up as far as the sky. There are two doors into the school. One has BOYS engraved in its stone lintel and the other has GIRLS.

The janitor has his own special house between the two playgrounds. I want to know what's inside, but the bottom halves of the windows are frosted to stop children from peering in. I have to stand up on the stone wall and hold onto the railings and tip my toes as high as they'll go to see through the clear upper half. The wee house has just one room with a toty kitchen, a fireplace, a tartan armchair and a board on the wall that has more keys than I've ever seen dangling from its hooks. There's writing that tells you which doors the keys open, but from where I'm standing on the wall, it just looks like black marks.

During the day the janitor is mostly in the school. When it's time, he comes out and rings a brass handbell to tell everyone to get into line. He comes out of the boys' door to ring it in the boys' playground and then, like the wee wooden people in the weather house we have at home, he goes back into the school and comes out of the girls' door to ring it a second time. Sometimes, if he's in a good mood, he lets one of the boys ring the bell. I watch them through the railings and long to be the one with the wooden handle in my fist, feeling the power of the swinging metal, making the noise that gets everyone running to line up. The janitor doesn't let the girls ring the bell.

Not on the first day, but later on, when I'm used to school and have trodden the path often enough to walk home on my own, we have our first lesson in writing. I'm ridiculously excited. This is what I want to do more than anything.

One of the girls in the front row is given a pile of brand new, school-blue jotters. She moves up and down between the rows of desks, putting down one book at a time. I wait for my own book to arrive. The pages are creamy white with faint blue lines running across, and a red vertical line down the left-hand side. They smell of holidays. On the matte cover there's a single word, *NAME*, and some dots to show you where to write it. I pick up my pencil and I write my name and I'm so pleased with what I've done that I tilt the cover towards the boy sitting next to me to show him. He looks at the jotter and his eyes narrow. He turns towards the front of the class and raises his hand in the air, sitting taller in his seat to make it go higher.

A tiny trapdoor opens in the bottom of my stomach and a small, cold stone drops into the pit of me. I know I've made a mistake, but I don't know what it is. The teacher says *Yes, Stephen?* to the boy and the boy turns to look at me and then he points so there can be no mistaking who has done this terrible thing.

SHE'S written on her book, he says.

I look round anxiously to see if it's true that you're not supposed to write your name in the space for your name, but the children's faces are blank, waiting for the teacher's reaction. When I turn back to the teacher, I can see the answer. Her face has darkened like a rainy day and clouds have gathered behind her glasses. In a low rumble she tells me to bring my book to the front of the class. I pick it up and make my way slowly between the desks. The teacher holds out her hand and I give her the book. She looks at it. She holds it up to show the class. Her other hand snaps round my wrist and pulls my arm up. *Look!* she shrieks. *Look at what this stupid girl has done!* I start to cry. *What is wrong with you?* she demands. *It should be me that's crying, not you. Why have you ruined this book?*

It said NAME, I whisper.

What? shrieks the teacher. *What did you say?*

I cry harder. *I thought it was the space for my name.*

Did I tell you to write your name on your jotter? Her voice crackles like broken glass. *Did I tell you to do that?* she says again when I don't answer.

No, I whisper through my tears.

NO! she repeats loudly, like an angry parrot. *NO, I DID NOT! I haven't taught you how to write your name yet. When I have taught you how to write your name, then you'll be allowed to put it on your jotter.*

She lets go of my wrist and orders me back to my seat, but that's not where I go. Instead, I make straight for the classroom door. I run down the corridor into the girls' toilets and I lock myself in a cubicle and cry and cry into the crisp, non-absorbent paper that the school has provided for children to wipe their arses.

When I've stopped crying, I leave the toilets. I don't go back to the classroom, I run home, but when I reach the end of my street I stop. I've done something really bad. If I go home early, I'll have to tell my mum about this bad thing I've done. Maybe she'll be angry like my teacher. I sit down on the kerb with my feet in the gutter and I wait until I see other children coming back from school, then I go up to our flat. I pretend that nothing has happened.

———

After this, I begin to have recurring nightmares that include a sprite-like creature called Jack Frost. The dream can start off quite pleasantly: a picnic, a playpark, a game of hide and seek. Then Jack Frost appears. Suddenly I realise I'm on my own. I can see my parents, but they're far off in the distance; they don't know what's happening so they can't help me. Jack Frost raises an icicle wand and points it towards me. I try to run, to call out to my parents, but he's too quick for me. He laughs, and it's the sound of broken glass. The wand crackles and I'm instantly frozen. I'm powerless, unable to move. I try shouting again, but my voice turns to ice in my throat and nothing comes out. *Nothingnothingnothingnothing.* I wake with the panic-stones rattling in my chest, crying out for my mum.

My mum knew about the Jack Frost dream, but I never told her what the teacher had said to me. Of course, as an adult I know that I did nothing wrong. I know that the teacher should have congratulated me on my initiative, not punished me for it. I also know that my mum's anger would have been directed towards the teacher, not me. I can imagine her storming up to the school to complain, the small, quick steps she took when she was annoyed, her fists held tight in against her sides. She would have made certain that I knew I had done a good thing, a clever thing, that it was the teacher who was at fault. It's a shame I didn't speak up, that I didn't give her the opportunity to defend me. It's more shameful that I was made to feel I had done something wrong. I thought the teacher, by virtue of the fact that she was the one in charge, must be right. I was mortified at the thought that I had broken the rules and upset her.

That was the first time I kept quiet about someone hurting me because I felt ashamed. That's the first thing I remember learning at school.

because we're taught as children to respect authority, because those in power are the ones making the rules, because those in power want to stay in power so they make sure the rules are in their favour, because we're taught that girls shouldn't speak out about achievement, because after the age of five girls narrow their visions for the future, stop wanting to be scientists, explorers, astronauts,[1] because we're all channelled into gender-specific behaviours, by example, by history, by media, by the toys we're given and the stories we're told, because Barbie and all her pretty dresses, because Action Man and his uniforms and weapons, because damsels in distress and princes to the rescue, because don't throw like a girl, scream like a girl, cry like a girl, because sugarandspice sugarandspice sugarandspice, because slugsandsnails slugsandsnails slugsandsnails, because forcing gender expectations on children leads to long-term mental and physical health problems, whether they're boys or girls, because the myth that boys are strong and independent while girls are vulnerable and nurturing is a global one, perpetuated throughout the world[2]

CHAPTER 3

He's there again.
The second time I met
The Man (auction house)

After the email from The Man, I avoided the auction house. I felt funny about going there. I didn't want to see him again. But a couple of weeks later, something came up that I wanted to bid on. I hadn't had any more emails and I was beginning to think I had overreacted. Looking at it logically, he hadn't done anything wrong. He hadn't threatened me or been offensive. A little over-eager maybe, a little too personal, but, as my partner said, probably nothing to worry about. There was a good chance he wouldn't even be at the auction house, and if he was, it seemed unlikely he would speak to me. I hadn't replied to his email—he would surely have got the message.

On the day of the auction, I cycled across town and parked my bike under the metal staircase outside the warehouse doors of the auction house. I waited while two men manoeuvred (with much shouting and swearing) an enormous stone fountain through the doorway. They were rolling it on its side, like a giant wheel. It kept veering off in one direction or the other, crunching over toes (hence the swearing), picking up momentum when it hit the slope outside the door and careering wildly towards an Alfa Romeo (much hollering and more profanity).

Inside the building, the bidding was in full flow. It looked busy. The dealers were gathered together at the back of the room, most of them middle-aged men who had been in the business for years. They all knew each other. Gales of laughter punctuated their conversation. They seemed to know intuitively when a lot they were interested in came up. They blithely carried on their conversation while raising a hand to bid. I was deeply impressed by this. Whenever I knew one of 'my' lots was coming up, I would get jittery and anxious. My heart would start thumping and I would suddenly, desperately, need the loo. I'm not sure what it was that made me so nervous. The idea that I might get it wrong, that it might turn out to be the wrong thing or that I could end up paying too much for it? I wished I could be as nonchalant and relaxed as the dealers.

I stood at the back for a few minutes, scanning the room for The Man, but there was no sign of him. Feeling more at ease, I moved closer to the podium, to watch the bidding. I'd been standing there less than five minutes when I felt someone's breath, hot and damp in my ear, a rasping whisper, *I know what girls are into.* I turned around, the hairs on the back of my neck literally standing on end. His face was inches from mine. I staggered backwards and he must have seen the horror on my face. *Hey,* he said, *I was just referring to the title of your poetry book.*

I surprised myself with the bluntness of my response. *I'm aware of that,* I said coldly, *I just don't like people sneaking up on me.*

He drew himself upright, and looked down at me, frowning. *I wasn't 'sneaking up',* he said. *You're being paranoid. And you didn't answer my email. I sent an email to . . .* he reeled off my email address . . . *but I didn't hear back from you.*

Okay, so what I should have said was, *What? Why did you send me an email when I told you I didn't think it was appropriate?* Or, *Yes, I got that email, but I didn't reply because I don't want any contact with you.* Or, *STOP sending me emails and STOP whispering in my ear. In fact, could you just keep the actual fuck away from me.*

But I didn't say any of those things. I didn't want to be impolite. I didn't want to cause offence or make a scene. And there was something about the way he was looking at me. I could tell he was angry, but it wasn't just that. A voice inside me was saying, *Be careful. He's dangerous.* So instead what I said was, *Oh, that's an old email address, I don't use that one anymore.*

Ah yes, he said. *I thought that must be what had happened. Well here's what I said to you.* He repeated the email verbatim. *And I've read your book now, cover to cover. I'd love to speak to you about it. When can we meet for a coffee?*

I took a step back, away from him. *I can't meet you for coffee*, I said. *I have a partner.*

It's just coffee, he said, laughing.

Again that look. A kind of sneer. I felt pathetic but I couldn't shake the sense that there was something weird going on, something deeply wrong with all of this. I stood in silence trying to work out how to leave without angering him further.

He tried to start up the conversation again. *I was thinking about you the other day*, he said. *I was in Prospect, looking at a house. Maybe you know it. It's an old stone cottage that someone's doing up. There's a pile of bricks outside it. I'm interested in the way they've done the pointing. I'd like to do something similar with my house.*

Rattling stones of panic. The cottage he was describing was directly opposite my house. Was he playing some kind of game? Was he trying to tell me he knew where I lived? He carried on talking about the cottage, how he'd spoken to the owner about the pointing. I wasn't paying much attention. All I could think about was how to get away from him. I got my phone out, making a show of looking in my calendar. *I'm sorry, but I need to go*, I said.

He did that drawing himself up thing again, looking down his nose at me. *But you just got here.*

I know, but I have an appointment I forgot about. I just got an alert.

He stared at me. *Okay,* he said, *I'll see you later.* The words themselves were casual, but the tone was menacing, his mouth a thin, straight line, his eyes flat and cold. I turned quickly and made for the door.

———

I was ridiculously unnerved by this interaction. Was it ridiculous? That business with the stone cottage was certainly odd. I was convinced The Man was threatening me in some way. I felt sure he wanted to harm me, but maybe that was quite a big conclusion to jump to, based, as it was, on

In the pub

After a night out in Adelaide's CBD, a friend and I head for the railway station, hoping to catch the next train. As we hurry along the pavement, my friend checks her phone for train times. It turns out we've just missed one and we'll have to wait another fifty minutes for the last train of the evening. We slow our pace and decide to nip into the pub across the road from the station for a last drink. It isn't the sort of pub either of us would normally choose to go into because

a) it's a sports bar

b) it has pokies and

c) most of the clientele are men

but it's also

a) close to the station

b) open late and

c) cheap.

We find a table beside the floor-to-ceiling windows that look out on the station, the casino and the groups of (mostly) drunk people who are making their way along North Terrace. We're deep in conversation when two men in suits come over.

Hi, says the one in the grey suit, *I hope you don't mind us approaching you like this but we're visitors here and we're wondering if you can help us. Can you tell us where the best restaurants are?*

Depends what you're looking for, says my friend. *What kind of food do you like?*

Well, says Grey Suit, *I like all sorts of things. Indian, Chinese, Thai.* He pulls a chair over from a nearby table and sits down next to her. His friend in the navy suit does the same, drawing his chair alongside mine.

So what's YOUR favourite restaurant? he asks.

A familiar sense of discomfort pokes at the edges of me. Not just irritation at the conversation hijack but also a feeling of mild coercion. My friend and I want a quick drink and a chat before the train leaves. The Suits are after something different and we've somehow been manoeuvred into joining in with what they want. It doesn't seem as if there's any polite way to redirect them. I start blathering on about how I'm the wrong person to ask, because my partner and I are generally more interested in child-friendly restaurants on account of our three bairns. Poor Navy Suit. He knows there's no point carrying on, but Grey Suit is still engaged, chatting and laughing with my friend. We make half-hearted attempts at small talk while we wait it out.

Eventually The Suits leave. Five minutes later, a man with a ponytail and leather jacket lumbers towards us, slopping beer from the pint glass he's holding. *Ladies, ladies,* he says as he approaches, *you've saved me life. All me mates have left. I went to the pisser, came back, they were gone. Thought that was me night over but now here you are, waiting for me. Do you mind if I join you?* He wavers on his feet.

Sorry, mate, I say, *we're actually about to leave. Train to catch.* At least he asked.

No worries. He seems to have expected the knockback. He turns around and slops off, puddles of beer in his wake like footprints.

I'm beginning to wonder if we've accidentally stumbled into a singles bar. Why are all these men so sure we're sitting here waiting for male company? Something to do with the proximity to the red light district? Or just late-night desperation?

We try to resume our conversation, but now a group of four drunk lads are cavorting around on the pavement outside our window. They're laughing and waving at us, taking swigs from bottles of beer, slapping each other's backs, holding each other up. The whole evening has become so farcical that we start laughing, too. One of the young men purses his lips and holds his palms towards the window, making and unmaking claws of his fingers, pretending to be either an aggressive cat or someone squeezing a pair of boobs. Another mimes giving a blow job to a dildo/dismembered cock/exceptionally tall man. I stare through the window at the four of them, caught for a moment in their nasty tableau. Then, half-joking, half-serious, I roll my eyes and give them the finger.

Instantly the tableau dissolves. *Fuck you!* they yell at us, their faces twisted into sneers. *Ugly lesbian bitches!*

One of them drains the bottle of Fosters he's carrying, then hurls it straight at the window. I leap as it hits the glass right in front of my face, my heart wrung with panic. Fortunately, the Great Goddess of Health and Safety is smiling down on me: the bottle bounces off the reinforced glass, leaving us unharmed. The men take off down the street.

I'm mortified. I apologise profusely to my friend. *I'm so sorry*, I say. *That was totally my fault. I shouldn't have wound them up like that.*

She looks at me, astonished. *Are you seriously apologising for what they just did? Don't DO that. That was NOT your fault.*

I know it isn't entirely my fault. I don't think I was 'asking for it', but I do feel the situation could have been avoided if I'd ignored them, that I should have been aware of the potential for aggression. I feel at least partly responsible for not playing by the rules.

because the rules tell us it's up to us to protect ourselves, because we're taught to be careful, because we're taught how to behave in order to avoid unwanted attention, because sugarandspice sugarandspice sugarandspice, because it's always our fault, because if we wear high heels, short skirts, low-cut tops we're asking for it, because if our breasts are large we're doubly asking for it, because if we cut our hair short, wear jeans and Doc Martens we're ugly man-haters who are also asking for it, because we shouldn't be walking the streets alone at night, because we must arm ourselves with rape alarms, pepper sprays, bunches of keys, self-defence classes, because we're teaching this to our daughters, because we feel this is the only way to keep our daughters safe, because if we are walking the streets at night, any man or group of men we see becomes a potential threat, because we're told they can't help themselves, we're told it's just the way they are, because boys are told the same thing, slugsandsnails slugsandsnails slugsandsnails, because this nursery-rhyme polarity isn't working for anyone, because this is just stating the bleeding obvious, because even though it's bleeding obvious it's STILL HAPPENING, because 'I can't believe I'm still protesting this shit'[1]

CHAPTER 4

Trying to escape
The Man

I stopped going to the auction house. It was annoying that I was having to give something up because of The Man, but it also felt like taking control. If I don't go there, he won't be able to speak to me, I thought. If he sends any more emails, I can just ignore them. I don't have to interact with this man if I don't want to.

Initially, I was still anxious—I thought there might be a chance he would appear near the house—but after a couple of weeks it started to feel like I had been getting worked up about nothing. I hadn't seen him, he hadn't tried to contact me, I thought that must be the end of it.

In fact, it was just the beginning. Or rather the middle. This was when I met him in the park after dropping my son off at school. This was when he told me he recognised my trousers, and that he knew I had changed my routine. This was when I first realised he was a cyclist and it became white-light bone-shakingly apparent that I was being followed. Why else would he be here? How else could he know *I* would be here, in the park, at this time? I had convinced myself I was overreacting, but he was back again, confirming my initial fears. It was a huge shock. I couldn't help wondering if he'd timed it deliberately, waited until he thought I would be more relaxed and off-guard before making an appearance on my home turf. Was he actually TRYING to scare me?

During the 1990s Balkan conflict, my brother worked for Edinburgh Direct Aid, a charity in Scotland that sent lorryloads of food and emergency supplies to civilians in Bosnia. He and seven other drivers drove a convoy of articulated lorries to and from Britain and the Balkan states. On one of the trips, they got stuck in Sarajevo. The city was being heavily shelled and a convoy of huge artics could easily become a target. He and his colleagues waited it out in a tiny flat in a high-rise block at the centre of Sarajevo, all eight of them in sleeping bags on the living-room floor.

The shelling was intense. The drivers stood at the windows of the flat looking out across the city as shells exploded and buildings fell apart in a whoosh of orange flame and roiling clouds of smoke. It was terrifying. The high-rise block shook with the impact of nearby shells. You never knew if the next one might be coming for you. It was psychological as well as physical warfare. The attacks, often at night, were timed to create maximum terror. *Bang . . . bang . . . bang . . . nothing . . . nothing . . . nothing . . . bang . . . bang . . . nothing-nothing-nothing-nothing-nothing-nothing-nothing-nothing-nothing . . .* You would just be starting to relax, my brother said, would just have convinced yourself that that was it, it was over, when the shelling would start up again . . . *bang . . . bang . . .* Everyone was ragged from lack of sleep. Nerves were shredded; they fizzed and sparked like loose electricity, sometimes jolting into arguments. People were having to live like this. Not just for a few nights, but on and on. Month after month. No escape from the fear, the saw-scraped anxiety.

I thought of those people when I saw The Man in the park. How easy I had it compared to the intense suffering of being trapped in a war zone. I could hardly imagine carrying on with that level of fear and no hope of escape, what it must do to you, mentally and physically. It seemed ridiculous to even contemplate it in connection with my own situation but I couldn't help wondering if The Man was using similar tactics, deliberately trying to create maximum anxiety by strategically planning his appearances.

All of this was running through my head as we walked. The prim suburban streets on the other side of the park were quiet except for the unsyncopated rhythm of our footfalls and the frayed shrilling of the noisy miners in the leaves above us. For some reason I had taken my rucksack off my back and was carrying it in front of me, hugged into my chest. I hadn't been aware of shifting it, but I somehow felt comforted by the solid weight of computer and books held against my body as the man pushed his bike alongside me, chatting away as if we were old friends. I couldn't bring myself to turn my head and look at him as he talked. I kept my eyes fixed on the ground ahead of me. Smooth grey tarmac scattered with leaves and petals. Raised bumps and cracks where tree roots had pushed through.

As you can see, I'm a cyclist too, he was saying. *It's my primary mode of transport.* The phrase sounded strangely familiar. *The reason I'm in this area is because I wanted to have a look at a house in _____ Street.* He named one of the streets that was quite near the park. He described the house. I knew it, I passed it every day on my way to and from my son's school. *I'm thinking of doing my garden in the same style,* he said, *so I've come here to have another look at it. It's just up here. After I've seen it I'm going into the city to* _____ *café, do you know it?* I didn't. *It's a vegetarian café so I often have lunch there. You should go there sometime. You're vegetarian, too, aren't you?*

Yes, I said. *Yes, I am.*

On the outside, I was behaving as if all this was perfectly normal, but pennies were starting to drop, their sharp edges biting into my skull.

He knows I'm vegetarian. I haven't told him this. I'm pretty sure there's no mention of it online. How can he know?

And that comment about the bike being his *primary mode of transport.* It was the same phrase I had used when I introduced myself on the stage of the 'Big Bike Brekkie'—*I'm not a lycra cyclist but I cycle every day; my bike is my primary mode of transport.* That was why it sounded familiar. Was it possible that this man had first seen me at the 'Big Bike Brekkie', that he'd been standing nearby when I attempted to get a vegetarian breakfast, that he had followed me to the auction house and then back to my home? Was he dropping these hints deliberately because he wanted me to know he had been following me, wanted me to know he was the one in control? On the inside, I was freaking out.

because he knows my daily routine, because he's a cyclist, because he knows I'm vegetarian, because he might have been following me, off and on, for weeks, because I knew nothing about it, because I can't DO anything about it, because if he wants to follow me I can't stop him, because this story about the house with the garden is almost the same as the other story about the cottage across the road from my house, because if he knows where I live he might know who my children are, because he could start following them too, because maybe he already has, because sometimes men bundle women into the backs of vans, because Jill Meagher, because Jill Dando, because Eunji Ban, because Eurydice Dixon, because Renea Lau, because Jo Cox, because Natalina Angok, because of all the others, all the not famous women who don't appear in the media, who get killed for saying the wrong thing, for being in the wrong place, because tiny stones of panic, inside all of us, rattling, rattling, rattling

We went past the house he had described. I had expected him to stop and look at it, maybe to take photographs. It was going to be my get-out clause—*I need to go home so I'll leave you to it*—but he didn't stop.

He did speak about it as we walked by. *That's the house. You see how the garden has that really striking formality? It's very much a style I'd like to emulate.* More and more details about the house, why he'd had to travel across town to look at it. But he didn't stop to photograph it. He carried on walking beside me.

I got really nervous. Was he going to stick with me all the way home? I didn't know what was real anymore, couldn't work out if I was being paranoid, imagining things, freaking myself out unnecessarily. On the surface he was behaving so casually, so normally, yet every atom in my body was screaming at me to get the fuck away from him.

———

Since then, I've read Gavin de Becker's *The Gift of Fear*.[1] In it he describes several behaviours that indicate the person you're talking to could be dangerous. 'Forced teaming' is one, where someone you barely know attempts to establish a rapport by assuming or manufacturing a connection. (I'm a cyclist, just like you. I'm vegetarian, just like you.) Giving too many details is another, an indication that they're lying. When someone is telling the truth, they expect you to believe them, but when they're lying, they're usually worried that you'll realise, so they try to sound more believable by adding extra detail to their stories. There's also 'typecasting', where the person delivers a slight insult that is designed to make you try and disprove it (e.g. telling someone they're stubborn/suspicious/paranoid in order to get them to behave in a more trusting way to prove that they're not). And then there's the 'unsolicited promise' ('I promise I won't hurt you', when that's exactly what they're planning to do, or maybe 'I'm not trying to find out where you live . . .'). But the biggest indicator by far is a person discounting the word 'no'. When you say no and the other person doesn't seem to hear it, it's because they want to control you, says de Becker. The worst thing you can do is give in to them, because it lets them know they're the one in charge.

Our gut instinct will kick in when this sort of thing is going on, he tells us. We sense that something isn't quite right. This happens when our body realises there's no time for careful evaluation and it moves into fight-or-flight mode. Our eyes and ears pick up the tiny clues and send them straight to the amygdala, bypassing the cortex, the thinking part of the brain, so that we 'know' and react without thinking. It's a valuable defence mechanism. The problem is that our modern culture has no time for intuition. Mystical woo-woo, it tells us. Cold, clear cognitive processes are far superior. And so we question, or even ignore, the instinctive warning signals, convincing ourselves that it's our imagination.

———

Those intuitive rattling stones had told me, from my first interaction with The Man, that something was wrong, but I had shushed them by deciding that I was being paranoid, that it was all in my head. This time, however, the fear and horror overwhelmed me and the further I walked with The Man, the louder the stones rattled.

We came to the last main street before my suburb. If we crossed over it and carried on, we would end up in parkland. Probably deserted parkland with huddles of trees and bushes, the sort of place where women get attacked. I did not want to cross the parkland alone with this man. I stopped and turned towards him.

If you're going into the city I guess you'll be going back that way, I said.

To my relief he nodded. *Yes,* he said, *I'd better go. Nice talking to you. I'll hopefully bump into you again sometime.*

At work

Just recently, I told my friend something I'd never told anyone else. I hadn't intended to tell her. We were talking about the #MeToo movement and I found myself saying, *I've never experienced actual sexual abuse* . . . Then I paused. *I can't believe I just said that*, I continued. Years of conditioning.

I'm in my early twenties, working as a waiter in a restaurant bar in Edinburgh. My boss tells me he needs to pick up supplies from another restaurant. He wants me to come and help. We get into his car and travel across town to Lothian Road. On the way we chat and joke around. My boss is ten, maybe fifteen, years older than me but we get on well together. He likes to tell me stories of his life back in Italy. The idyllic island, orange trees by the side of the road, he and his friends as young boys, picking the fruit on their way to the beach, the juice running down their chins, chasing each other into the surf to wash it off.

We arrive at the 'other restaurant', which is really more like a café. Counter down one side as you go in, big silver coffee machine, a row of booths on the other side, the seats covered in red vinyl. My boss ushers me into a booth. My thighs, in their black nylon tights, slide along the seat. He asks if I'd like a coffee and I tell him a cappuccino would be lovely.

He goes up to the counter, where three other men who work in the restaurant are standing talking. They greet him with loud cheers, bear hugs and back slaps. They have a raucous conversation together, laughing and exclaiming. One of them leans back with his elbows on the counter and shakes out his long, curly hair. They're speaking Italian, so I only catch a few words. Ragazza. Ristorante. Rigolo. At one point they all burst into song. 'Nessun Dorma'. The Three Tenors were big at the time.

Eventually one of the baristas goes behind the counter. The coffee machine hisses and gurgles. Steam billows as he cleans out the milk wand. My boss returns briefly with my cappuccino, then goes back to his friends. I sit skimming the chocolatey froth off the top with a teaspoon, glancing up at the men, who sometimes glance back at me.

Suddenly more back slapping and *ciao, ciao.*

My boss returns. *Let's go*, he says. I leave my half-drunk coffee on the table and trot out after him, my heels clacking on the ceramic floor tiles. We get back into his car. We go to a different restaurant and it's the same routine. He sits me at a table, brings me a coffee, talks with his friends, then we leave. Back in the car, I'm not sure what's going on but I'm too embarrassed to ask. I assume he hasn't been able to find what he needed and we're either going to a different restaurant or back to the restaurant I work in, but instead he pulls up outside a tenement building in Tollcross. He gets out of the car and opens my door.

Where are we going? I ask as I get out.

This is Gianni's place, he says. *I need to get something.* Gianni is one of the other waiters at the restaurant where I work. He's my boss's nephew, a year younger than me, very good looking, very flirtatious. We've kissed a few times, in the storeroom at work, and once he came back to my flat when we'd finished our shift. He's currently on holiday in Italy.

I follow my boss up the internal stair of the tenement, my shoes slipping on the shiny dip at the centre of the steps where the feet of the last two centuries have worn the stone away. We arrive at the front door of the flat, which he opens with a key. It's a smallish flat—living room/kitchen, one bedroom, bathroom—but it's cosy, nicely furnished with throws, cushions, pictures. There's a fluffy cardie on the back of the sofa, men's and women's jackets and scarves hanging by the front door.

Did you know Gianni had a girlfriend? my boss asks.

No, I say, *I didn't.*

She lives here with him, my boss says. He picks up a fat pink notebook from a shelf under the window. *This is her diary. You can read it if you don't believe me.*

I shake my head.

Come with me, I have something else to show you, he says. He leads me through to the bedroom. I hover in the doorway, uncomfortable about being in someone else's private space. My boss isn't uncomfortable. He opens a bedside cabinet and pulls out a magazine, throws it on the bed. *Come on,* he says, *come over here. I want to know what you think of this. This is the kind of thing Gianni's into.*

I walk over to the bed and look down at the magazine. It's a sort of comic, black-and-white strip cartoons that tell the story of a woman being gang raped at knifepoint. Close-ups of her terrified face, the men's nasty grins, their erect penises shoving into her.

I don't remember what I said. *It makes me feel sick*, maybe. Or *Why are you showing me this?* I remember the nausea. I don't remember the words. And I can't equate the toxic porn with Gianni's cheeky, boyish smile, his careful hands, his soft words, even if he has kept quiet about his girlfriend.

I turn back to the door, wanting to leave, but my boss moves in front of me and shoves me backwards onto the bed. I fall onto it with a thump, crushing the magazine. He climbs on top of me. Not in an aggressive way—he's almost playful, laughing as if we're play-fighting. I struggle to break free. I'm not playing. Rattling stones of panic. I want him to get off me and keep saying so. *Stop it, please, let me go!*

He isn't nasty or threatening but he's forceful, cajoling. *Come on, you want this, you know you want this.*

I don't want it, you're hurting me, please stop.

You don't want me to stop.

I thrash around under him, but I can't get away. *Let me go, you're scaring me, please, get off me.*

He laughs down at me. He has me pinned by the wrists, his knees holding down my thighs. He lets go of one wrist and yanks at my clothes. My arm flails wildly, hitting him, pushing at him. He grabs my wrist again, twists it. *Come on, now*, he says. *Don't be like that.*

Eventually I give in. It seems pointless fighting back, and I just want it to be over. Tears run into my ears as he thrusts himself into me. He doesn't look at my face, he looks straight ahead, grimacing.

Nnngh, nnngh, nnngh.

Cold, hard, distant.

Even when he's finished, I can't stop crying. I straighten my clothes. A button is missing from my blouse and the gusset of my knickers is ripped and flapping. I try to hold it in place with my tights.

What are you crying for? my boss asks irritably as he zips up his trousers. *It doesn't make any sense. You liked it. It was good.*

I want to scream at him—*it wasn't good, it was horrible!*— but I don't. I just keep crying. When we're both dressed, we go downstairs, get into his car and go back to the restaurant. He chats away as we drive, as if nothing has happened. I go back to work. I finish my shift. I go home and shower and I cry a bit more, but it doesn't occur to me that I've been raped. Until very recently, I wouldn't have described it as rape. Until recently, I wouldn't have spoken of it at all. I was ashamed. I thought I was complicit in the filth of it: I had been too friendly with him, I was wearing a short skirt and heels, I must have been giving him the wrong message, I didn't struggle enough, I gave in. Somehow, I thought, it must have been my fault. Years of conditioning.

———

In *Axiomatic*, Maria Tumarkin talks of the Greek tyrant Histaeus, who wanted to get a secret message to Aristogarus.

Histaeus shaved the head of one of his trusted slaves, tattooed the message on his scalp and kept him hidden until all the hair grew back. Then he sent him to Aristogarus, who shaved the slave's head again to reveal the message.

All the messages tattooed on our scalps. All the hair we've grown over them.

'The existence of the secret message is a secret,' writes Tumarkin. 'We don't know to go looking. Perhaps telling and not telling are not what we think they are. Perhaps experience could be placed in narrative for safekeeping, hidden in it, not to be buried or rendered unknown, but to be preserved so as to be revealed in a different kind of story.'[2]

because my boss didn't see this incident as rape, because I didn't see this incident as rape, because I also pretended that nothing had happened, because I carried on working for him, because this must have confirmed to him that there was nothing wrong with what he did, because I didn't want to make a scene, because I didn't want to lose my job, because he was the one in charge, because I felt like I must have broken the rules, because I was ashamed, because the patriarchy uses many different mechanisms to ensure women internalise the desired social norms,[3] because I'd been brought up in a culture that told me I wasn't supposed to complain, because the culture is still telling me not to complain, because don't be a Karen, because women have internalised so much that we're unconsciously helping to support misogyny, because one in seven young Australians think it's okay to rape a woman if she initiates sex, then changes her mind,[4] because rape is now recognised as a weapon of war, because the UN says that it has become more dangerous to be a woman than a soldier during a war,[5] because people sometimes think certain types of rape are just normal sexuality, because normal sexuality has historically been defined from the male point of view, because we need to be aware of the type of gender politics that create an environment where sexual abuse can be normalised, because we need discussion and education more than we need punishment, because the answer is to listen to each other, because although listening is difficult (especially if it means changing behaviour, changing long-held beliefs, admitting fault, giving up power) we can't move on without it

CHAPTER 5

Reaching home after escaping. Increased anxiety

When The Man cycled off, I didn't wait to make sure he kept going. I raced down the street, desperate to get away as fast as I could. I kept looking over my shoulder. The idea that he had been following me around for weeks without me knowing made me feel stupidly naïve, like Little Red Riding Hood, skipping through the forest with her basket of goodies, unaware that a wolf was creeping through the undergrowth beside her.

I cut across the parkland with my heart ricocheting around my rib cage.

The sun had come out and the sky looked like the opening credits of the Simpsons—cerulean blue, little fluffy clouds. A flock of corellas was gathered at the side of the path, making contented chirruping noises as they pecked the ground beneath the trees. More corellas bounced on the branches above, releasing little puffs of sweet-smelling yellow pollen from the catkins. It was pretty much an Australian version of *Bambi*, yet my head was filled with more ghoulish images: The Man loping over the grass towards me, his ears growing pointier, his teeth lengthening, body dropping low, large tongue lolling and slavering, claws scarring the earth as he bounded across it. My overactive imagination filled my whole body with terror, propelling me faster and faster towards the comparative safety of my own suburb.

I felt a moment of relief when I made it to my house and shut the door behind me, but my certainty that The Man knew where I lived meant I couldn't completely relax. I dropped my bag on the sofa and sank down beside it. I was sweating. I got back up again. I paced around the living room.

What to do, what to do.

I felt so powerless. I wanted to be able to take control, but I didn't know how. Maybe Google would give me some answers. I got the laptop out of my bag, opened it up and typed in, *What to do if you have a stalker.*

Bad plan.

Most of the websites that came up were American. *BUY A GUN!* they said. *These people are HIGHLY DANGEROUS and POTENTIALLY PSYCHOTIC! You need to take the threat SERIOUSLY! Convert one of the rooms in your home into a PANIC room for you and your family! Make sure you can LOCK AND BARRICADE it from the inside! Keep your passport, your bankcards, your important documents with you AT ALL TIMES so you can leave the country IMMEDIATELY if you need to!*

By the time I'd finished reading, I looked like Munch's *The Scream.* I prised my rigid fingers from the side of my head and phoned my partner at work. *That man! The one who sent me the weird email! He just met me in the park! I think he knows where I live! I think he's been following me!* Gibbering like a lunatic, I told him what had happened, what had been said.

Okay, said my partner, *I think you need to report this to the police. Why don't you come and meet me at work? We can go to the station together.*

Relieved that I had something positive to do, relieved that my partner was supporting me and I wasn't alone, I went to the shed in our back garden and got my bike out. I wheeled it around to the front of the house then went back inside for my bag and my bike helmet. Helmet strap fumble. Spike of panic when I couldn't remember where I'd put my bag. Eventually I was ready. I shut the front door behind me and checked up and down the street. There was a car parked in the space outside our gate and someone was sitting in the driver's seat, looking at their phone. I took a couple of steps up our pathway and bent down to peer through the passenger window. I snapped upright and leapt back.

It was him.

It was definitely him.

The Man was sitting outside my house, waiting for me.

At a poetry reading

It's the early nineties and I'm excited. I've been invited to read at a literary event in Edinburgh alongside Irvine Welsh, Irish poet Brendan Cleary and a few others. This is pre-*Trainspotting*, so Brendan Cleary is the headline act.

I spend a bit of time choosing poems and working out a set. On the night, I meet a couple of friends for drinks in the Barony Bar, then we all head along to the Broughton St venue.

The room is hoaching with young Edinburgh literati. A writer I know, a novelist who has had a couple of books published by Bloomsbury, waves to me from the other side of the room. He's sitting with a friend of his, a poet called Pete, who's also going to be reading tonight. Pete and I know each other but we haven't spoken much. I wave back, but I don't go over for a chat. I had met the novelist for coffee a few months previously. He'd said he was 'a big fan of my work' and wanted to publish a couple of my poems in the magazine he wrote a column for. He also wondered if I wanted to join a writing group he was part of.

You should come along next Thursday, he said. *It should be a laugh. There's a woman there called Marian, she's a lezzer, and she's always reading out really bad, man-hating poems. So on Thursday I'm going to read out a poem I've written called 'The Hack-faced Slag Who Needs a Good Shag'.*

I told him it didn't really sound like my kind of thing.

Since then, I'd sent him the poems and, true to his word, he'd published them in the magazine. We hadn't met up again.

My friends and I find a table in the middle of the room and sit down to listen to the readings. It's a great atmosphere, plenty of buzz, a good supportive crowd. There are four of us reading in the first half, then there's a break, then it's Brendan Cleary. I'm third up. I've tried to choose the crowd-pleaser poems, ones that generally get a good laugh. A couple are relevant to the story, so I'll quote them here. They were written in phonetic Scots but I've included a translation.

TIME AND AGAIN

thi cloak	the clock
oan thi waw	on the wall
sezits timety	says it's time to
get thi bairnz reddy	get the children ready
get thi hoos tidy	get the house tidy
get thi messijis in	get the shopping done
get thi tee oan	get dinner made
get inty bed	get into bed
an gie um hiz conjuggles	and give him his conjugals
thur wizza time when	there was a time when
I . . .	I . . .
naw thur wizny	no there wasn't

ELLIS GUNN

TAKING OFFENCE

he sayz	he said
gawn hen	go on, love
geez a feely	give us a feel of
yur tits	your tits
ah sayz	I said
awane huvva wank	go and have a wank
or it leest	or at least
thats whit	that's what
ah woody sayd	I would have said
sept ah thot he mite be	except I thought he might be
uffendit	offended

The poems seem to go down well and I return to my seat on a wave of applause. I'm buoyed by the reaction, floating in a bubble of confidence as Pete gets up on the stage. He leans into the mic. *Ellis Gunn,* he says to the audience, *always a hard act to follow. And a great pair of conjugals on her, and all!*

I'm completely gobsmacked. What have my boobs got to do with my performance? Without thinking I shout out, *Awane huvva wank, Pete!*

It's met with a roar of laughter from the audience. Pete looks crestfallen. *I think I'll save that for later,* he mutters, but it's a weak comeback and he's uncharacteristically flustered on stage. Tattoos itching beneath my hair, I feel a bit of remorse for having made him uncomfortable. Years of conditioning.

Other than that, it's a great night. Brendan Cleary's reputation as a fabulous performer is well deserved. He leaps around the stage, using different voices for the characters in the poems, delivering his set with a sense of fun and upbeat energy that has the audience roaring and gasping with laughter. Afterwards, we're all buzzing. We move on to a pub for some late-night drinking.

Some of the male writers, Pete and the novelist included, sit in a tight cohort at one of the tables. A couple of times, I think I see Pete and the novelist scowling across at me. Maybe I'm being paranoid. Brendan Cleary is sitting with them, but at one point he gets up and comes over to me and my friend Caroline standing at the bar.

I'm about to head off, but I just wanted to say I loved your set, he says to me, *and I'm sorry about that shitty remark that was made afterwards. You shouldn't have to put up with that kind of nonsense when you're performing your work. Totally disrespectful.*

I shrug it off. *Och, it happens,* I say.

Aye, it does, says Brendan. *But it shouldn't. And I felt like you deserved an apology.*

Well, it shouldn't be you who's apologising, but thanks, I say. *I appreciate it. And I loved your set, too. Amazing work.*

He waves shyly as he moves off. *Thanks,* he says, *catch you later.* And he disappears out the door.

Wow, says Caroline, *what a lovely guy!*

I nod in agreement and take a glug of my beer. Over the rim of the pint glass, I can see Pete bumping his way through the tables towards us. *Hey,* he's saying, *hey, Ellis.* He's fairly pissed.

Pete, I say, nodding to him.

Hey listen, he says, *that was a bit much, what you did there. I think you were maybe misunderstanding what I was saying.*

I laugh. *Well, what I did understand was that I was reading out my work, which I take fairly seriously, by the way, and your response was to make a comment about my boobs.*

Naw, naw, naw, he says, *see you've got me wrong there, that's not what I was saying, not at all, so there was no need for you to be a cunt about it. You've had the Cleary fella tearing a strip out of us. All of us that are sitting at the table there,* he jerks a thumb over his shoulder, *he thinks we're a bunch of arseholes, thanks to you.*

I want to say, *Thanks to yourselves, more like,* but I hold my tongue. I actually like some of the people Brendan was sitting with. In any case, Pete has finished what he's come to say and is making his way back across the pub. Caroline doesn't remark on what a lovely guy he is. She says something quite different.

———

A couple of things happen on the back of this. The first is that the novelist writes a review of one of my chapbooks and publishes it in the journal he writes for. Despite having published my poems a few weeks before, despite having said he's 'a big fan of my work', he absolutely slates it. Ordinarily, I might have been upset by a bad review, but I think I know what this is about. It seems too petty to stress over.

The second is that I get invited to read at another event in an art gallery in Cockburn Street. Some of the same crowd are there, including Pete, although he's not reading this time. There are only a few chairs at the back of the room, so most of the audience sit on the floor. I stand at the front to read, and halfway through my performance, Pete stands up and says loudly, *That's me away for a wank, then!* He gets a laugh from the crowd and swaggers out of the room, stepping over the legs of everyone seated on the floor.

Unfortunately, I don't have the nerve to actually say what's on the tip of my tongue—*I always knew you were a wanker.* Instead, I just raise my eyebrows, shake my head and carry on with my reading. The last thing I want is to start a slanging match, or some kind of vendetta where we're both trying to get the better of each other at every poetry reading. Besides, I've been taught to take offence, not give it.

because woman as object, because on three separate occasions in the last year I have been walking along the pavement, past a café with outdoor tables, and have happened to be behind a young, slim, conventionally attractive woman, because on each occasion several men sitting at the tables have literally turned in their seats to follow, with their eyes, the young woman as she walks on down the street, because lots of people would be baffled as to why there's anything wrong with that, because woman as object, because when any female celebrity of a certain age is mentioned, a cousin of mine (a man I love and respect) will comment on how beautiful she is, and I know he thinks he's championing women by saying they can still be beautiful even when they're middle aged, because a woman's main purpose is to look good and everything else is secondary, because woman as object, because on the British panel shows I like to watch, the host is almost always a man, the team captains are almost always men, because one of these shows has a 'glamourous assistant', a woman with a degree in mathematics from Oxford University, who is regularly sexualised when she is introduced, because she smiles and laughs along with the comments about her body and the enjoyment male viewers get from looking at it, because women still have to play by the men's rules, because woman as object is one of the rules

CHAPTER 6

Going to the police to report the stalking

I stood on my front path, frozen with terror. I felt completely trapped. I couldn't possibly leave the house when The Man was sitting there in his car, waiting for me. But was staying in the house any safer? What if he tried to get in? I had no alternative; I went back inside and phoned my partner again. *I can't leave,* I whispered into the phone, *he's outside in his car. He's waiting for me.*

Stay there, my partner said. *I'll come and get you.*

I paced up and down in the kitchen while I waited for him to arrive. My body was fizzing with anxiety, primed for flight but caged by fear. I almost screamed when I heard my partner's key turn in the lock.

Hello, are you okay? He came into the kitchen and wrapped his arms around me. *I just had a look in the car outside,* he said. *There's no one in it now. I think I've seen it parked there before, though. I thought it belonged to someone who worked nearby.*

Oh my god, he's been here before? I said. *How often has he sat out there, waiting?*

Let's just go to the police station, my partner said. *Are you okay to go in on the bus, or do you want me to drive?*

We can get the bus, I said. *I'll be okay as long as I'm not on my own.*

At that time my partner worked in a building close to the main police station so that was where we went. It was the first time I'd been in a police station in Adelaide, though it wouldn't be the last. There was a woman at the counter when we went in. We waited as she spoke to the police officer behind the desk, telling her about the breach of an injunction order. I tried to look like I wasn't listening, but it was difficult in such a small space. Details were taken and she was asked to take a seat. It felt so public, having to report intimate life problems with an audience present. I was nervous and close to tears as I stepped up to the counter. *A man has been following me*, I blurted out. *I think he's a stalker.* Thankfully, the officer behind the desk was understanding. She asked questions and listened patiently to my answers.

You think he was in a car outside your house? she asked.

Yes, I said. *I'm pretty sure it was him. We took down the registration number.*

Okay, she said. *We'll get someone to check it out. If you could just take a seat until an interview room is free.*

My partner waited until I was called into the interview room, but then he needed to go back to work for a meeting. The room was small and divided in two by a desk that separated the public side of the room from the police-station side of the room. It was painted grey and white. I sat down in the grey chair on my side of the desk. A police officer came through a door on the other side of the desk and sat down opposite me. Like the officer out front, he was extremely considerate and reassuring. There was no suggestion that I was being hysterical or imagining things. He was taking me seriously, which filled me with gratitude and relief.

I was able to tell him the name of The Man, or at least the name he used for his email address. The officer looked him up on the computer that sat to his right. He spun the screen round to show me a photo. *Is this him?* he asked.

———

Years later, when I'd written the first draft of this book and my agent was pitching it to publishers, one of them asked me why I didn't google The Man, why I didn't try to find out more about him, why I didn't follow him back, see what he did, where he went. By this stage, I was sufficiently distanced from the experience to see that this might seem an obvious course of action, but if she'd asked me the same question at this point, I would have stared at her in amazement.

In fact, my partner did google The Man and was able to verify that some of what he had told me was true, at least according to what it said online, but there was no way I could have done this myself. I simply COULD NOT bring myself to type his name into my computer. I couldn't even bring myself to SAY his name. I don't know how to explain this level of fear. It seems completely counterintuitive. The best example I can come up with is, if you suffer from arachnophobia you're probably not going to type 'big hairy spiders' into Google to see what comes up. All my energy was focused on NOT thinking about The Man, all my instincts said, *Danger, danger, run, run.* FOLLOW him?! I desperately wanted to keep as far away from him as possible.

Even there in the police station, the image of The Man's face on the computer caused something dark and clotted to creep into my stomach.

Yes, I said, swallowing, *that's him.*

As I went through the details, all the things that had been said and done, from the very beginning, I felt foolish about how much I'd given away. *I don't know why I told him so much about myself,* I said. *I was really stupid.*

Not at all, the officer assured me. *These people are practised at getting information from others. And from the age of this guy, I'd say it is highly unlikely that you're the first person he's ever stalked. He's probably refined the art. He's probably very good at what he does. You shouldn't be blaming yourself.*

He spent a few minutes checking the police database. *Sorry,* he said as we waited, *the system is really slow.* And then, after a while—*Well, the good news is he doesn't have any convictions, at least not in South Australia.*

I don't think he's been in South Australia very long, I said. *At least that's what he told me. He said he'd recently been divorced and had moved here from Sydney. I don't know if that's true.*

The officer told me he wouldn't be able to access the New South Wales database. *But let me have a look at that registration number,* he said, *I can find out if it's his car.*

I passed him the bit of paper with the number and car make written on it, and he tapped it in. He found the car, but it wasn't registered to The Man. It belonged to someone else.

I was shaken. I had been so sure it was him that I'd seen sitting in the driver's seat. Maybe he'd borrowed the car from a friend. I was starting to doubt myself, though. I had been quite far away and it hadn't been easy to see inside the car. If I'd imagined this, what else might I be imagining? My brain felt like a thick soup of fear and confusion. Was I going mad?

At the end of the interview, the officer assured me that they had The Man's address and could get in touch with him if they needed to. *At the moment, he hasn't done anything that would warrant an arrest or even a caution*, he said. *I know it's frustrating, but that's just the law.*

I understand, I said. *I wasn't really thinking he would be arrested. I suppose I just thought I should register it.*

The officer said it was good that they knew about it and that I was to keep them updated with any further developments. I didn't feel any safer when I left the station but at least I had been listened to sympathetically. The most frustrating thing was that I still didn't know if The Man had any previous convictions for stalking or, indeed, any other crimes. For all I knew, he was a human trafficker, a mafia boss, a mass murderer. The fact that he hadn't been convicted of anything in South Australia was hardly a comfort when he had only just arrived here. Why wasn't there some kind of national database that the police could access? Surely it would help victims (and the police) to know how much of a threat the pursuers were. I couldn't be the only person to have seen this flaw in the system. Why had nothing been done about it?

———

Later, when I was in the process of writing this book, I spoke about this to Ann Moulds, founder and CEO of the Action Against Stalking Centre in Glasgow. She explained that the situation wasn't unusual. 'One of the main issues that police have in dealing with stalking is that it doesn't follow the same retrospective paradigm that most crimes do,' she told me. 'The police are used to investigating something that has been done, rather than a dynamic crime like stalking. And if it's difficult for the police to access criminal records, they're not going to take the time to do that unless they think a serious crime has been committed.' Because of this, Ann has worked tirelessly to get stalking recognised as a separate (and serious) offence in Scotland, the UK and Europe. Her advocacy led to the *Victims and Witnesses Act 2014* in Scotland, which was a huge step forward in the recognition of victim's rights. The act focused on the reaction of the victim and allowed behaviours to be deemed criminal if they resulted in fear and alarm for the victim. This didn't need to be objective—it was all about the victim's perception, which was crucial.

Criminal analyst Laura Richards is also working to get laws changed in England and Wales. She has drawn up a

24-page report[1] detailing links between serial stalkers, serial coercive controllers, those who murder women outside of the home, and terrorists. She argues that, in many cases, serial murders and acts of terrorism can be predicted by looking at domestic violence and stalking histories, and that it's therefore imperative that serial domestic violence and stalking perpetrators go on the Violent and Sexual Offenders Register so that their case histories can be monitored and future violent crimes prevented.

I asked Ann if she felt a stalkers register might be a useful tool. Here's what she told me: 'Without a doubt, for serial stalkers, we've got to have a register, but we need to be careful about who goes on that register. Sometimes, due to unusual circumstances, people find themselves engaging in stalking behaviour out of desperation. It's not something they've done before and might not be something they'll ever do again. Those people don't need to be on a register. And to my mind, there's not enough knowledge out there, in the police force, in the criminal justice system, about stalking and the nature of stalking, to make those decisions. We need to build up our knowledge of different typologies of stalker and work out who needs to be on the register and how long for.'

In my mailbox

We've been living in our house in Prospect for a few years. I have a small business doing interior design and I'm now also renovating and selling up-cycled furniture. Today, I'm on my driveway, working on something for a client, a large reception desk that's too big and heavy to move round the back where I normally work. A man in a baseball cap appears at my gate and pops something into the mailbox. He raises a hand and calls out a cheerful good morning as he carries on up the street with his bag of leaflets. I wave back and carry on painting. Then I stop, put down the paintbrush.

I've just remembered something disturbing that I found in our mailbox a few months previously, a leaflet from a 'Christian' organisation that said gay people were the spawn of Satan and were all going to drown in the fiery vomit of God's wrath. Or something like that. The views expressed were so extreme they were like a ridiculous spoof of themselves. Nonetheless, it felt intrusive, this hate speech appearing in our mailbox. It could have been that the organisation was just leafleting the whole neighbourhood (it WAS at the time of the marriage equality 'survey') but it just so happened that there was a 'Vote Yes' poster in the front window of our house, so it did feel like we might have been targeted. What really ripped my knitting was the thought that it could quite easily be a child or teenager who came across these leaflets. Did the people posting them realise how damaging this kind of hate speech could be to a young person? I felt compelled to tear the thing into tiny pieces before putting it in the bin.

So, as I put down the paintbrush, I'm wondering if the man in the baseball cap is the same person who delivered the previous leaflet. If he is, I want the opportunity to voice my concerns. I go and have a look in the mailbox. It turns out the leaflet isn't some crazy anti-gay thing, it's some crazy anti-abortion thing. Vivid pictures, loaded language, the works. As someone who firmly believes that it's a woman's right to determine what happens to her body and her life, it kind of gets my goat. I march to the end of the street, looking for Baseball Cap. I have no idea what I'm going to say if I find him but I'm damn well going to say something. I walk to the crossroads, look left and right, and spot him posting leaflets in a street on the other side of the park. I stride towards him, leaflet quivering in my fist.

Excuse me, I yell out as I approach.

He looks up. *Yes?* he says amiably. *Can I help you?*

I still haven't worked out what I'm going to say, so I improvise. *You can help me by not posting this shit in my letterbox*, I say, handing him back the leaflet.

Ok, he says, *no problem*.

I turn on my heel and walk back to my house, feeling shaky and sick and stupid. *What was the point of that, you idiot?* I say to myself. *What did that accomplish except making both yourself and him feel bad?*

I try to work out what rational me might have said. *I see from this leaflet that your views are very different to mine and I'd like to find out why, so . . .*

1. *Why are the rights of a foetus more important than the rights of a fully formed woman?*
2. *Who's going to take care of the unwanted child? Would you? If it would persuade someone not to abort, would you agree to look after a child, care for it for the rest of its life?*
3. *Do you think it's okay to kill civilians in a war? Why would it be okay to kill a fully formed person or a fully formed child but not okay to terminate a pregnancy, something that isn't even a person yet?*

I could already hear his responses:

1. *Abortion is killing a person; I'm not talking about killing the pregnant woman.*
2. *It's the woman's responsibility to take care of the child, not mine; she's the one who got pregnant.*
3. *Civilians in war are collateral damage for a greater purpose, not deliberately killed because they're inconvenient.*

And my rejoinders:

1. *When a foetus is aborted, it isn't a person yet, but you ARE talking about dictating what the woman is allowed*

to do with her body and the rest of her life—why is that up to you?

2. *It takes two people to get a woman accidentally pregnant and, in any case, doesn't everyone make mistakes? Should smokers also be denied treatment for lung cancer because they've brought it on themselves?*

3. *How can you be prepared to call the death of fully formed people justifiable collateral damage but the termination of a pregnancy unconscionable murder?*

And so on. The conversation might not have made either of us change our minds, but at least I would have expressed my views calmly and rationally, I would have asked him to justify his. That's got to be better than rage, right?

Maybe. But later, when I listen to Shankar Vedantam's podcast *The Hidden Brain*,[2] I realise that rage is not an unusual reaction in situations like this. Neuroscientist Doug Fields points out that there are a number of situations that cause animals to respond with rage and violence: when their own lives, or the lives of their offspring, are in danger, when their resources (food or territory) are under attack, or if they feel trapped. Humans are also animals and we respond in the same way. Just as de Becker explained in *The Gift of Fear*,[3] Fields says that, when we're in a threatening situation, there often isn't time to think our reactions through, so we've developed high-speed pathways that send signals to the amygdala before they go to the cortex (the thinking part of the brain).

Rage is the 'fight' reaction designed to save us from danger. More significantly, animals and humans can also react with rage when they see a threat to social order. We need a stable, functioning society in order to survive and we're willing to fight to maintain order or to correct injustice.

If rage is a normal, instinctive reaction to injustice, why do I feel such a sense of shame whenever I have an angry outburst? Have I been conditioned to police my own rage, and is this a good or a bad thing? In *Rage Becomes Her*,[4] Soraya Chemaly points out that men generally experience anger as powerful, while women associate anger with power-lessness. This could be because girls and women have long been denied the right to express their anger and have their views listened to respectfully. While white male anger is often portrayed as justifiable and a show of strength, women who get angry are generally seen as loud, demanding and out of control. 'Anger has a bad rap, but it is actually one of the most hopeful and forward thinking of all our emotions,' Chemaly writes. 'It begets transformation, manifesting our passion *and* keeping us invested in the world. It is a rational *and* emotional response to trespass, violation and moral disorder. It bridges the divide between what "is" and what "ought" to be, between a difficult past and an improved possibility. Anger warns us viscerally of violation, threat and insult.'

She further points out that bottling our rage is neither good for us nor does it make us good people. It neither protects our interests nor helps us challenge corrupt systems.

One thing it IS good for is minimising the complaints of the oppressed, thereby maintaining an unjust status quo.

Oxford University philosopher Amia Srinivasan[5] agrees. Anger can be clarifying, she says. It can help an individual understand when something isn't right, by sending messages to the brain that can lead to moral and political understanding. And it can also act as a warning signal to other people. Contrary to traditional liberal ideas that calm deliberation is the only real mechanism for change, there's a lot of social and psychological evidence to suggest that anger can be an effective means of communicating a message to others and motivating them to change their behaviour.

I know I didn't handle the situation with Baseball Cap in the best way I could have, but maybe I don't need to be so hard on myself for expressing my anger. Maybe the anger needs to come out, needs to be expressed and heard, before real change can begin to happen. As Sheryl Ring says in *Burn It Down*,[6] stay angry for long enough and eventually it could turn into the fuel you need for creativity and resistance.

because self-blame is a common response for women, because we've been taught, in many subtle ways, to find fault with ourselves, because we've been taught that anger is righteous and powerful when expressed by men but hysteria when expressed by women, because we've been taught that an angry woman is a crazy woman, because the ongoing undermining, the mansplaining, the objectification, the repetition of what you just said as if it were the speaker's idea cause a build-up of anger and frustration, because the anger is often met with disbelief when expressed, so you learn not to express it, because not expressing anger can impact the immune system and cause long-term health issues such as chronic pain, rheumatoid arthritis, cardio-vascular disease and cancer,[7] because misogyny and sexism is literally making women ill

CHAPTER 7

Stalking and its toll on my mental health

I don't remember what I did after I left the police station. At some point I must have gone to school to pick up my son. I must have taken the bus home with him, because I would have been too afraid to walk that route again, my mind still full of the horror of my earlier encounter. I must have made dinner for everyone and we must have sat around the table and eaten it together, and all the time a bell must have been ringing loud and insistent inside me *somethingiswrong-somethingiswrongsomethingiswrong* and I must have shut my mouth around the sound, which would have been easy, because I've had lots of practice. It's what I've been taught to do. Easy, at least, until everyone else went to bed.

I remember I couldn't go to bed because it was too dark. It was dark outside and it was dark in the house and there was a creeping darkness inside me, a giant ink stain spreading across the blotting paper of my brain. I was scared of the dark, of what it was hiding, scared of the dark thoughts ploughing their dark grooves into my neural pathways. I stayed up and tried to distract myself with reading, and when the words went into my eyes but refused to cross into my ink-stained brain, I tried again with television. Still no use. The things I'd read on the internet kept popping up and waving their hairy arms, gnashing their broken teeth.

When I was younger, I thought everyone was good. I believed, with the black-and-white certainty of youth, that people only did 'bad' things because they'd had bad things done to them, and if they were treated with kindness and understanding, their badness would be polished away and goodness would shine through. This philosophy survived a series of flashers, survived a violent relationship, survived all the everyday incidents of harassment, and even survived rape. But somehow the stalking experience shattered it. *There are people out there who are psychopaths*, I told myself. *And if they come after you, there's nothing you can do about it.*

Wrapped inside the dark and quiet of the sleeping house, what I felt more than anything was alone. The house was no longer my safe space. I was suddenly very conscious that it was penetrable, that my body was penetrable.

A smashed window, a crowbar, a bottle, a knife, fingers, a needle, a prick.

I couldn't protect myself, the system couldn't protect me, my partner couldn't protect me, nobody could. And nobody seemed to understand. I was alone in the dark with an overwhelming sense of powerlessness. I tried going to bed, crawling under the covers beside my partner, careful not to waken him. I pulled my knees up to my chin and held myself small, but the hairy arms and gnashing teeth wouldn't stop. I couldn't make them stop.

I got up again and started pacing and my partner woke up and said, *Hey, are you okay?* and it was as if his voice came from very far away and didn't mean anything. He watched helplessly as I sank to my knees, lowered my head as if in prayer, combed my fingers frantically through my hair, over and over and over and over. Overandoverandover-andover. *I* watched helplessly, too. I was inside and outside myself. Inside was a balled-up mush of screaming madness. Outside was a sane person looking on, incredulous. *What on earth are you doing? Stop that, you look ridiculous, you're BEING ridiculous!* But I couldn't stop. My fingers combed and combed as torrents of anxiety poured out of me.

because nowhere is safe anymore, don't you see, because here he comes and here he comes, because I can't stop him, I can't stop this, there's nothing I can do, nothingnothingnothingnothing, because someone is probably going to die and I hope to god it's me and not one of the children, because I've been stupid and unwary and it's my fault, because now we have to go, we have to leave, we need to get away, go back to Scotland, because danger and danger and danger for everyone, all of us, anytime, anywhere, everythingeverythingeverythingeverything

My partner got up and came towards me and tried to hold me, and it should have been a comfort, to feel that connection, that love and support, but it wasn't. I was the eye of a furious storm, bloodshot, unblinking, speckled with grit from the tornado of dirt that whipped its frenzy around me. I felt myself falling into my own dark pit, fear ribboning out above me in a long, soundless scream. I was such a whirlwind I couldn't be contained, I had to break free.

I'm sorry, my partner said as I pushed him away. He was visibly shaken by my distress. *I really want to help but I don't know what to do. It's like you're broken and I don't know how to fix you.*

Talking to a schoolfriend

I'm sixteen, still at school and living at home with my family in Edinburgh. It's Saturday today and my friend Sarah has popped in to see me. We're in my bedroom, talking. She's sitting on my bed and I'm cross-legged on the floor, facing her. Bowie's *Scary Monsters (and Super Creeps)* is playing on my stereo, appropriately as it turns out.

Sarah is in the year above me at school, which would normally make me feel quite shy, but she's just about the sweetest person I've ever met, kind and gentle, easy to talk to. She's also very beautiful, with a wide open, smiley face and a froth of blonde curls. At the moment her beauty is badly impacted by the purple and green swelling that has turned her left eye into a puffy golf ball with a closed slit in the middle. She's taking some time off school, she says, until the swelling goes down. She's embarrassed, doesn't want to be seen like this, doesn't want everyone going on about it.

Sarah is going out with an older man. His name is Trent and he's in his mid-twenties. He's her best friend's brother. Her best friend's parents have gone overseas for work and they've left Trent to mind the house and look after his younger sister. Every month or so, they have a big party that lots of the older students at school go to. I've been to a few of them, which is how I got friendly with Sarah. She's been going out with Trent, off and on, for as long as I've known her. They're always splitting up and getting back together again.

Sarah is telling me how she got the black eye. During one of the periods when she and Trent had split up, Sarah was seeing one of the biology teachers at school. Her best friend was seeing the other one. They used to go out together in a foursome. They were supposed to keep it secret, but loads of people knew about it. Sarah said it felt good going out with a teacher, even though she didn't really fancy the one she was with. He was bald with a beard. The one her best friend went out with was a bit better looking but still old. She didn't really like either of them, not the way she liked Trent, but it made her feel grown-up. It made her feel 'like a lady' was what she said.

Eventually, Sarah and Trent got back together again and she stopped seeing the biology teacher. She didn't tell Trent about the relationship, but he had found out about it a couple of days ago when someone dropped her in it. He went mental. He called Sarah a slut and a whore. He made her tell him all the things she'd done with the biology teacher and then he said she was disgusting and he couldn't bear to look at her and he punched her in the face and told her he wanted nothing more to do with her.

Oh my god, HE gave you the black eye? What a complete arsehole! I say to Sarah. *You're definitely better off without him.*

Sarah looks sheepish. *We're actually back together again now*, she says. She says she thinks Trent's jealousy proves that he loves her, that's why he got so angry, because he can't bear to think of her with anyone else.

I'm aghast. *But he said all those awful things to you. And he hit you. How could you want to be with someone who hit you?*

Sarah squints at me through her one good eye. *Because I love him,* she says.

I don't understand. I don't see how you can love someone who's so horrible to you. I think she's being really naïve, but I don't say anything; I just stare at her eye, swollen shut beneath the bruise. I can see how awful it looks, but she can't, not without a mirror.

because we're so used to living in a culture of victim blaming that we can blame our friends or even ourselves when we're the victims, because as early as 1980, linguist Julia Penelope spoke about 'agency deletion' (the way we use passive language to talk about 'how many women are raped', not 'how many men raped women'),[1] because this encourages the view that women are responsible for the violence dealt them, because they should just leave, because they shouldn't walk home alone, because they should be careful what they wear/ how they act/ what they say, because agency deletion is still common practice, because Jane Gilmore is still trying to 'fix it', because sound bites and clickbait mean we're often presented with stories about men's violence against women that downplay the man's part in it, because '"Traumatic" and "humiliating" attack on girlfriend may end athlete's career',[2] because 'Woman stabbed during fight with man in supermarket carpark',[3] because 'Baby taken from NSW home at knifepoint'[4]

CHAPTER 8

Women being silenced, a panic attack and a trip to Victim Support

My partner was right. I *was* broken. It was as if all the years of belittling, manipulating and intimidating had finally gotten the better of me. The Man was the straw that broke the camel's back, the razor that shaved the slave's head so that all the tattoos were suddenly visible. I was very conscious of my vulnerability, my powerlessness. The safe world I believed in had collapsed around me like a fold-down house and I was standing alone inside the debris like Buster Keaton in his window frame.

Those sites of demolition are such lonely places. I know my partner was expressing his own sense of powerlessness when he said I was broken. He wanted to help. He'd been brought up in a society that told him men needed to take control, that it was a man's job to protect his partner and his family, and he hated not being able to do or say something that would make everything okay. But that same society had frequently told me my emotional reactions were unreasonable, hysterical, and so I thought he was saying this was my fault. I thought he was saying I was making all of this much worse than it needed to be, and it was because something was wrong with me. I didn't want my partner to think of me like that, I didn't want to be the mad woman in the attic, so I decided to stop telling him about my crazy thoughts. We could hardly avoid the topic of the stalker altogether, but I needed to keep my worst fears to myself if I didn't want to risk him thinking of me as a lunatic.

However, as Rebecca Solnit puts it in 'Cassandra Among the Creeps', 'Silence, like Dante's hell, has its concentric circles.'[1] In the days that followed, I struggled to keep a grip on things. When I was active or in company it wasn't so bad, but being alone was terrifying. Thinking had become an activity akin to entering a war zone where guerrilla thoughts hid behind benign ones, hand grenades with pulled pins sizzling in their fists. I found it impossible to escape into novels or poems, my old haunting grounds. My brain was too unfocused, too liable to jump from fictional world into the possibility of a horrific reality. Instead, I became addicted to Spider and Wordscape, meaningless puzzles that engaged my brain in functional activity and kept it away from guerrilla territory.

Night-time was the worst. I continued to have difficulty sleeping, and for the first time since I was a child, I had recurring nightmares. As with the Jack Frost nightmare, I could be having a perfectly pleasant dream, out in a restaurant with friends, or going for a walk, when I would need the toilet. The toilet set-up was always the same: a row of unisex cubicles with a thin wooden partition between the cubicles and the public space. I'd be sitting on the toilet when I'd hear someone outside. I'd look up and realise I hadn't shut the door properly, so I'd lean forward to close it in case whoever it was thought the cubicle was unoccupied. Just as I was shutting it, the person outside would start to push it open. I'd try to say, *Hey, there's someone in here*, but it would just come out as an incoherent stammer. I'd think, *It's okay, they must have heard me and realised I'm here*, but instead of apologising and moving away, whoever was on the other side would push harder. They knew I was inside, but they didn't care, they were still coming in. I'd push back frantically, vocal chords straining as I desperately tried to scream. I'd know there were lots of people on the other side of the wooden partition; if I just screamed loud enough, they'd hear me and come and help. But my vocal chords wouldn't work, my voice would be stuck in my throat, and this person was much stronger than I was—I couldn't keep them out. There'd be a splintering sound as the door hinges broke and I'd see the hands of the other person, the meaty, dark-haired fingers gripping both sides of the door, pushing it in on top of me. I'd feel its weight, squeezing out all my breath, and the fear, holding my voice tight in my throat. *Relax*, I'd tell myself, *just relax and you'll be able to call out*. That's when I'd wake up.

———

At the time, I thought the nightmare was just about my fear of the stalker, but I wonder now if it was my subconscious telling me a bigger story. The story of what it feels like to be silenced, of being under attack, yet too afraid to speak out. Solnit also quotes Judith Herman's *Trauma and Recovery* in her article. 'Secrecy and silence are the perpetrator's first line of defence,' says Herman. 'If secrecy fails, the perpetrator attacks the credibility of his victim. If he cannot silence her absolutely, he tries to make sure that no one listens.'

A priestess in Greek mythology, Cassandra can be seen as a metaphor for the abused woman whom no one believes. When the god Apollo falls in love with the young Cassandra, he tries to win her favour by enabling her to see into the future. When she continues to spurn his advances, he gets angry and curses her, saying that while he cannot take back his gift, he'll make sure no one ever believes her prophecies.

Many women have experienced something similar and not just when trying to speak out about incidents of abuse. Saying anything about male misconduct or the patriarchy when in the company of men leaves one open to accusations of being a conspiracy theorist, of exaggeration, delusion or downright mendacity. Sometimes, if you're lucky, there's just an uncomfortable shuffle and a stony silence.

———

Although nights were the worst, daytime wasn't easy either. I was still afraid to be on my own in the house. *What if he's outside? What if he tries to come in? What if he wants to hurt me?* My place of safety and comfort was now a cage, a trap. I couldn't bear to wait there like a tethered sheep about to be slaughtered.

Fortunately, I was self-employed. I had a small interior design business which meant I could be flexible about my movements and make sure I wasn't working at home at the same time every day. After dropping my son off at school, I could go to a café or a library to work, somewhere public where I would be surrounded by other people. Sometimes I would go to a café near the school, sometimes one in town, sometimes I would go to a completely different suburb. I travelled by bus, or I cycled, or I walked. I made sure my movements were unpredictable. Whenever I walked towards a shop window, I scrutinised the reflection carefully to see who was walking behind me. Wherever I went, I was always looking over my shoulder, hyper-alert, primed for flight, adrenaline pumping. It was exhausting.

Not long after the episode in the park, I had taken myself into town, with all the usual detours and changes of transport. I was walking along Rundle Mall when I realised that the same man had been walking behind me for some time. He wasn't behaving oddly and I doubt I would have noticed he was there if my brain hadn't been on high alert, but I kept catching his reflection in the windows of the shops we were passing. Shop after shop, he was still there.

I could feel the fear scrabbling in my throat. I knew it wasn't The Man, but the fact that someone, anyone, could at any point decide to follow me had become a frightening possibility. I stopped and pretended to be looking at a window display. The man carried on walking. I turned to watch him through narrowed eyes, then darted over the road to a food court, keeping my focus on him in case he looked back and saw where I was going.

Once in the food court, I found the toilets and shut myself in a cubicle. I was shaking and confused. Even though my fear felt very real, logically I knew it wasn't right. There were hundreds of people walking along Rundle Mall. The fact that one of them happened to be behind me, happened to be walking at a similar pace, was nothing to be concerned about. What was wrong with me? Why was I suddenly so terrified by the everyday?

In her book *I Choose Elena*,[2] Lucia Osborne-Crowley explains this reaction: once again, it goes back to the old fight-or-flight response. The sympathetic nervous system kicks in when we sense danger, sending out a rush of adrenaline that increases heart rate and breathing and sends blood to our muscles, priming the body for either fighting or running away. Once the danger has passed, the parasympathetic nervous system takes over, slowing down heart rate and breathing, stopping the release of stress hormones and generally moving the body back into a calm and relaxed state. The two systems usually work in harmony to help the body cope in different situations, but trauma can upset this balance. The sympathetic nervous system can become overactive, triggering adrenaline rushes and panic attacks even when no real threat is present. The trauma of finding out that I was being followed had left my sympathetic nervous system switched on, ready to sputter into overdrive at the least sign of danger.

But of course I didn't know that at the time. I had no idea why my emotional responses to ordinary situations were so out of control. The one thing I did know was that I couldn't carry on like this. I was sure it was taking a toll on my health: the lack of sleep, the constant state of anxiety, the sudden bursts of anger or upset. I couldn't take it anymore and yet I couldn't make it stop. I needed help.

Sitting there on the toilet seat, I got my phone out and googled *Where to get help if you have a stalker*. I found an address for Victim Support, waited until I was calm enough to walk along the street without looking like a lunatic, and went straight to their office.

I was still in a state of panic as I walked in the door. I explained my situation to the person at the desk and I think my shaking hands and voice persuaded her that I needed to see somebody urgently. She told me to take a seat while she found out who was available.

A few minutes later a counsellor came and introduced herself to me. She showed me into a quiet, pastel-coloured room and we both sat down. She asked me to tell her what had been happening. As soon as I started talking, the swollen bubble of anxiety I'd been carrying inside me burst, and I became a hot mess of tears and trembles. Fortunately, there was a box of tissues on the table next to me. *I'm sorry,* I said, screwing tissue after sodden tissue into my fist, *I think this is because I haven't cried about any of this, and now it's all coming out. I'm sorry to be putting it all on you.*

What a relief it was to talk about what I was feeling with someone who could explain it all to me. To quote Solnit again, 'To tell a story and have it and the teller recognized and respected is still one of the best methods we have of overcoming trauma.' I had been so scared of being viewed as crazy that I had kept my worst fears to myself, even when talking to close friends, but occasionally I would get brave enough to tentatively approach the subject. *I think a man has been following me*, I might say. *I met him at an auction and then he turned up in a park near my son's school.* The response was mixed. Many people were sympathetic and wanted to know more. They would ask if there was anything they could do to help. But others had expressed surprise, even disbelief:

Are you sure you're not just being paranoid?

What are you so scared of? It's not like he's threatened you.

Maybe he just likes you and wants to spend time with you.

These comments were no doubt intended to reassure me, but in fact they just reinforced the feeling that I was going mad. The problem was, I WASN'T sure. Maybe I WAS just being paranoid. Maybe my fear WAS completely unfounded. And yet somehow I couldn't override my gut reaction with logic.

These confusions frequently arise as a result of stalkers' behaviours. In fact, the majority of stalkers never threaten their victims. While their aim might be to intimidate their targets, they can employ very subtle ways of doing this in order to avoid prosecution. As a result, the behaviour can appear quite innocuous to others, even though the implied threat is obvious to the target. I was convinced The Man had described the cottage directly opposite my house as a way of letting me know he knew where I lived, but to anyone listening from the outside, it would seem like an innocent remark, a coincidence. If I'd told them I thought it was actually an attempt to frighten me, it would just sound like paranoia.

The counsellor reassured me that my 'extreme' reactions were not madness and not irrational paranoia. They were perfectly normal. She thought the main trigger for these reactions had been meeting The Man in the park and realising that I had definitely been followed. She asked me to tell her a bit about my life before all this started and we spoke about my family, my friends, my lifestyle, my recent arrival in Australia and my homesickness for Scotland. She said it sounded like I had a positive world view and that I was used to trusting people, which might be one of the reasons that I had been so badly affected by this experience.

When something happens to us that upsets our world view and forces us to reassess strongly held beliefs, it's traumatising, she said. She went on to explain that because I was already having to cope with adjustment disorder (i.e. homesickness) it would be doubly hard to deal with this additional stress. *But it sounds like you have a strong support network,* she said. *That's good. That's very important.* I would find out later just how important this was.

Over the next few sessions at Victim Support, I discovered a lot about the way my brain was behaving. One of the things that was most difficult to cope with was the fact that I didn't really know anything about The Man. He wasn't an ex-partner or even a previous acquaintance. I couldn't tell what he was really like, what he might be capable of, with only a few short interactions to go on. My mind kept jumping to horrific possibilities. I found out that this too was normal, a nasty little trick that our brains play on us. Thanks to intuition, my brain knew there was a potential threat, someone acting strangely, and it was trying to protect me by making sure that I was hyper-alert to any danger. There were huge gaps in the information I needed to assess the risk, and my brain was programmed to fill in those gaps. Unfortunately, it was filling them with worst-case scenarios because it thought that was the best way to prepare me to defend myself.

We spoke about other areas of anxiety and, with the help of CBT (cognitive behaviour therapy), tried to disentangle my thought processes. The counsellor gave me a list of different 'patterns of thinking' to help me identify what my brain was up to when my thoughts started to feel out of control. Catastrophising, the tendency to exaggerate the likelihood that something bad is happening or is going to happen, was certainly a major feature (*someone is walking behind me—they must be stalking me*, or *I know this man has been following me—he's probably going to break into my house and kill me*). Whenever my sympathetic nervous system took over, I was 100 per cent convinced that what I was envisaging was pretty much inevitable.

Words can be dreadful little hand grenades, but find the right ones and they can also act as a shield. The word 'catastrophising' was a godsend. If my brain started to launch a barrage of terrifying thoughts, I could say to myself, *This isn't real, it's just your brain catastrophising*, and that simple phrase was usually enough to stop me collapsing into the churned-up mud of the emotional battleground. It wasn't always easy. My brain was desperate to make sure I was aware of potential danger, and I often had to wrestle it into submission. But if I caught an anxious thought early enough, being able to label the pattern and remind myself that it wasn't reality but a trick of the brain was incredibly helpful.

While travelling by train

I'm living on the Orkney Mainland, an island off the north coast of Scotland, but I travel south a couple of times a year to give poetry readings or workshops. This time I'm going down to Edinburgh on the train.

It's January, deep winter, and not many people are travelling. The carriage I get into is almost empty. There are seats available at tables, but I choose a double seat instead. I'm pretty unsociable when I'm travelling, and if the carriage gets busier closer to Inverness, there's less chance of someone sitting next to me if I'm in a double seat. I sit by the window, put my bag on the seat next to me and riffle through it, pulling out notebooks, pens, a novel, a book of poetry, everything I need for the next few hours.

I love this train journey. My three children are still young, and much as I adore the rough and tumble of being with them, I also love settling into the quiet of my own head as I'm transported to a new place, the forced aloneness of the journey, the precious time spent reading, writing or just watching the Scottish moorland rush by. It's a landscape I know intimately. At this time of year, the gnarled brown carpets of heather are frosted white, and occasional gusts of snow blow across the moor. I watch, with a deep sense of belonging, as the train rockets past craggy, snow-capped mountains, brown, peaty burns and pine trees outlined against the whitened moors like charcoal drawings. It's all as familiar to me as the landscape of my own freckled skin.

At one of the early stations, Altnabreac or Forsinard, a man enters the carriage. He's tall and broad-shouldered. Despite the cold, he's wearing a cotton shirt with sleeves rolled up to his bulging biceps. One fist grips the handles of a black Puma bag that's slung over his shoulder, and he hums to himself as he strides (there's no other word for the way he moves) down the carriage, glancing from left to right. When he reaches my seat, he stops.

Would you mind if I sat here? he asks, indicating the seat that my bag's on.

I'm taken aback. There are so many empty seats in the carriage, why does he need to sit next to me? I want to say, *Yes, I do mind*, but somehow I can't make the words come out of my mouth. Instead, I find myself muttering, *Sure, no worries*, as I collect all my things and huddle them into my lap.

He swings his bag up onto the overhead rack and thumps down beside me, spreading his muscular thighs wide, as if about to give birth to a large truck. He smells quite strongly of meat. I try to subtly move my legs away from his, pressing myself up against the window.

I like to make friends when I travel, the man says, turning towards me. His big mouth widens into a grin, showing his enormous teeth. *I like to learn about the place I'm in, the people who live here. You can probably tell I'm not from this country.*

I relax a bit. This might explain his unusual behaviour. Maybe it's just very different in his country, the people more open and sociable. I smile, thinking about my own reaction.

How terribly Scottish of me. So reserved, so utterly dour at the prospect of having to speak to a stranger. I need to lighten up, take the opportunity to learn something by having a conversation instead of burrowing my head in a book.

Is it very different where you're from? I ask.

Ha! SO different, he says. *This country is too grey. No blue skies, no sunshine. How can you bear all this rain? My country is beautiful, so warm and friendly, much better than here. You would like it. Are you married?*

Yes, I say, a little taken aback at the abruptness of the question.

I think maybe that isn't true, he says, pointing at my hand. *You don't wear a ring.*

Ah, well, TECHNICALLY I'm not married, I say. *But I've been with my partner for ten years now, so it's basically the same thing.*

Any children? he asks.

Three.

How many are boys?

One, I say. Again I'm slightly bewildered by the unusual phrasing of the question.

One is okay, he says. *Two would be better. Even better if it was all three.*

I smile. *I'm happy with the children I have*, I reply. *I don't think gender matters.*

You're wrong, he says. *Boys are better. In my family, all boys. I am the oldest and the strongest.*

I'm not sure how to respond to that. I turn to the window and look out at the windswept moors, the passing rubble of old stone crofts, their thatched roofs long since collapsed into the landscape, their fireplaces filled with drifts of snow. I try to imagine living in a country filled with sunshine. I try to imagine being so sure of myself that I could stride down a carriage and sit next to a stranger, tell them they're wrong when they express an opinion. I can't. I can't imagine it.

Tell me about your husband, the man says.

My husband? I say. *Well . . . he's nice. Kind. He works hard, but he's also a really good dad. We sort of share the childcare, we both . . .*

He stops me. *But does he make you happy?* he says.

Em, yes, we're very happy.

He opens his mouth wide and his laughter booms around the carriage. He nudges me with an elbow. *YOU know what I mean*, he says. *Does he make you happy? Does he satisfy you?*

I blink at him, speechless.

I think not, he says. *The men in this country, they're not even circumcised. So disgusting. I don't think they make women happy with their ugly penises like little grey worms.* He lifts a fist and wriggles his pinky. *You need a big man to make you happy, a man like me. You see how big I am? My penis—also very big.* He squeezes his groin and laughs loudly again.

I know it's just words, but I feel invaded. He's put the image of his penis in my head now, and it makes me feel unclean, violated, as if he had actually undone his zip and exposed himself to me. I'm not comfortable speaking to this man and I know now it's nothing to do with cultural difference. I'm pretty sure there's not a culture in the world where it's acceptable to boast about the size of your tadger to someone you've just met. I want him to go away. I want to change seats, but I feel trapped. I don't know how to get out without causing a scene, without causing offence. Instead, I paw through the pile of stuff on my lap until I find my novel. I open it up and pretend to be reading. As we pass through the next few towns, he hums to himself and drums on his thighs. Occasionally he asks me something and I give him a short, curt answer, refusing to look up from my book. Fortunately, it's not long before his station comes up and he exits the train, bag slung across his back. He waves to me from the platform as the train moves off. I don't wave back.

Alone again, I breathe more easily and the tightness inside me uncurls. I put down my book and look out the window. A herd of deer appear on the horizon, among them a stag, the candelabra of its antlers stark against the heavy, grey sky. They stop for a few seconds, to watch the train hurtling past, then move down the side of the hill in one long, flowing wave and disappear into a forest. Seen and then, suddenly, not seen.

———

On another occasion, I'm travelling the same route, but this time from Edinburgh to Inverness. As I'm sorting out my baggage and trying to find my seat in the overcrowded train, a squaddie gets on. In Australia you'd call him a digger. He's wearing camouflage and carrying a kitbag. He sits down in the one vacant seat at the table across the corridor from where I'm sitting. He immediately takes out his phone and starts a conversation with a friend. He's talking so loudly it's impossible for anyone in the carriage to ignore what's being said. He seems to be organising a night out, and from the one side of the conversation I'm hearing, I gather that he's just finished a long period of duty and his friend is filling him in on what's been happening in his absence.

The squaddie's next call is to his girlfriend. It starts off casual enough, though there's something about his tone that makes the sudden yelling unsurprising when it comes. He initially accuses his girlfriend of flirting with someone, but this quickly escalates. Soon, he decides she must have been sleeping with several people while he's been away. He calls her a whore and a bitch and a slut.

Stop lying to me, you fucking lying cunt, he says. *Do you know what I've fucking got? I've got a gun with me, and when I get back I'm coming straight round to yours and I'm going to stick the barrel in your fucking lying mouth and I'm going to ask you one more time what you've been up to and if you keep lying I'm going to blow your fucking stupid brains out, d'you hear me? Your fucking brains are going to be all over the wall and that'll be the last lie you ever tell.*

He hangs up, then glances round the carriage, as if just realising he's on a train. *Ah, sorry about my language there, folks,* he says in a surprisingly calm and contrite manner.

The carriage is packed, but nobody has said anything during the course of his violent outburst. Still nobody says anything. We all look down at our books or phones or magazines, probably thinking about the gun that he may or may not have in his kitbag.

I start to wish I had been able to stand up during his conversation, to lay a hand on his shoulder as I once saw someone in a club do to calm the aggression of a person on a bad trip. *Excuse me,* ideal me would have said, *sorry to bother you, I know you're on a call, but the thing is we can all hear you. Is it really fair to threaten your girlfriend like this?*

Ha! He probably would have told me to mind my own fucking business. And it's probably not a good idea to try and reason with a wildly aggressive person. And it probably wouldn't have made any difference. I know horrific things happen to young men and women who go into the army. I've read about new soldiers being 'blooded'—forced to shoot someone in cold blood—to get them ready for battle. I know the young squaddie has probably seen and heard things I can only imagine. I know he's the victim of a system that fosters an inhuman level of callousness and aggression in order to get people to do what is required. But I don't really know how to address that.

———

My third experience of Misogyny on a Train happens when I'm travelling back to Orkney from Glasgow. It's late on in the journey—we've almost reached Thurso, where the train terminates. The carriage has gradually emptied and those of us left are sitting in a box of soft yellow light with dark hunches of landscape hurtling past outside. I suddenly become aware of a conversation going on at a table a few seats down from me on the opposite side of the carriage. The two people at the table have been speaking for some time but I haven't been listening, I've been too busy writing. It's not what they're saying that catches my attention so much as a shift in tone. One of the people at the table is a young woman, maybe nineteen or twenty. She talks with a Scandinavian accent and looks like she's probably a backpacker. *I'm sorry, I find it tiring, speaking in English for so long,* I hear her saying. *I think I need to rest.* She shuts her eyes, leans her head against the window.

The man opposite her is middle-aged, old enough to be her father. He carries on talking, regardless of her shut eyes, regardless of what she has said to him, and his tone becomes badgering, insistent. *What we'll do when we get off the train, we'll share a taxi, I'll pay. If you're sure you don't want to sleep in my spare room, we can go to the youth hostel first and drop you off, okay? Then tomorrow I'll come and pick you up and we can go sightseeing.*

He carries on, listing all the places of interest he can take her to. He's a valuable companion, he's telling her, he's lived here all his life, he knows the best places to go. The young woman has opened her eyes again. She nods and smiles politely. Eventually she gets up and goes to the toilet.

I'm not sure what to do. Should I go over to the man, say something? What would I say? I can't decide if I'm over-reacting. I'm on my way home after doing a poetry workshop with prisoners in Barlinnie, all of whom had been convicted of sex crimes. My intuition tells me something isn't right, but maybe I'm prejudiced by my recent experiences. Maybe I'm projecting their crimes onto this man.

Finally I decide to try and speak to the young woman instead. I go and wait outside the cubicle until she comes out and I ask if she's okay. *I'm sorry for intruding,* I say, *it's just, that man at your table, is he bothering you?*

She laughs. *Not bothering really, but so tiring,* she says. *He sits down at the table and then he just keeps talking. He wants me to stay in his house, to save my money, but I don't think so.*

Aye, I say, *I don't think so either—you need to think about your own safety. He sounds a bit dodgy.* I feel as if I'm acting like her mother. I have a strong urge to make her understand her vulnerability, travelling on her own in a foreign country, but am I being patronising? I don't want to treat her like a lost child.

I think maybe he's just lonely, she says.

Well, as long as you're sure you're okay, I say. *I definitely don't think you should go anywhere with him. And you're welcome to come in a taxi with me instead. I'm going to the ferry terminal but I could drop you off first.*

I'll be okay, she says, smiling. *I'm sure he's not dangerous.*

———

I hope she's right. I think about her sometimes over the next few days. I check the news to see if there are any incidents of young women going missing in Caithness. I etch the man's face in my memory in case I need to describe him. I remember him calling the taxi from the train, that the taxi driver knew him. I wonder again if I was just being paranoid. Maybe, like me, he was worried about her safety. Then I think about his badgering tone, the fact that he had sat down beside her in the first place, that he wasn't listening to her 'no'. I feel tired, too, thinking about these men on trains, the ones who don't want to listen, who shout about what they want with apparent disregard for what other people need.

because when I said yes to the man who wanted to sit beside me, I was mixing up politeness with pleasing people, because girls still get rewarded for politeness and taking care of others while boys are more often rewarded for being brave and taking risks, because girls generally have a harder time communicating their preferences, because middle-school girls in particular tend to keep quiet about their wants and needs in order to fit in,[3] because cultural differences mean that women are more likely to communicate in ways that increase connection while men are more likely to communicate in ways that emphasise their independence or authority,[4] because this makes it easier for men to exploit women, often unconsciously, because managerial roles tend to favour male modes of communication, which makes it harder for women's voices to be heard, because the gendered use of language has been skewed so that it gives greater credence to male speech,[5] because maybe if we were all more aware of this it would help us think more about what we say and the way we say it, maybe it would make us listen more carefully, maybe it would help move us towards gender parity

CHAPTER 9

Has The Man been to my house? Implementing CBT

It took some time, and a lot of work, for the CBT to make a major difference to my fear of The Man. As is normal with PTS, the slightest trigger could flip my sympathetic nervous system into overdrive, sending me into a frenzy of anxiety.

One morning, I got back to the house after taking my son to school, and instead of heading up the driveway as I usually did, I went via the gate so I could check the mailbox. As I walked towards it, I could tell something wasn't right. The door on our side of the box, where you took the mail out, was standing open. I knew I hadn't opened it—I'd been in a rush when we left and hadn't thought to look for mail— and it would be very unlike my methodical partner not to have shut it after checking for post. In any case, I would have noticed if it was standing open when I left the house, and I was pretty sure it hadn't been, so someone must have opened it while I was dropping my son off at school.

Who would do such a thing? Had The Man been here? Had he TAKEN something from the mailbox? Was he trying to get more information about me? I walked up the path to the front door, fumbling anxiously for my keys. I put my bag down on the table next to our front door. As usual, the table was covered in a thick layer of dust, but today there were long stripes in the muck, as if someone had dragged their fingers across it. I stood frozen, staring at those sinister stripes. They looked like the claw marks of an animal who had marked its territory. Was this a message from The Man? Did he want me to know he had been here, that he knew where I lived and could get me any time he wanted?

By the time I got into the house, I was in full catastrophe mode. My breath was coming in short gasps and I was walking up and down, up and down, unable to calm myself. Was he out there now, had he waited to see my reaction? Fortunately, I remembered the CBT sheets that the counsellor at Victim Support had given me. After a bit more gulping and pacing I managed to persuade myself that it might be worth trying to fill one out. The sheet suggested that every time I felt overwhelmed with emotion I should write down:

1. What had happened
2. Which emotions had been triggered and how extreme they were on a scale of 1–5
3. What thought had provoked the emotions
4. Evidence that supported my thought and evidence that didn't
5. Alternative ways of thinking about the event/other possible reasons for what had happened
6. How extreme my emotions were on having completed the exercise.

I raked through the pile of papers on my desk and pulled out one of the sheets.

Despite thinking that it probably wouldn't change anything, I started filling it out:

1. The door of the mailbox is standing open and the table under the verandah has finger marks on it.
2. Fear, anxiety, anger, 4/5.
3. I think The Man has been to my house. I think he's been looking in my mailbox and has maybe even taken some of my mail. I think he left the door open, and his finger marks on the table, because he wants me to know he's been here.
4. Supports: the mailbox door is never open, we always shut it after checking for mail, and I would have noticed if it was open when I left the house, but I only saw it when I came back. I don't think the finger marks were there either and I can't imagine why anyone in the family would want to put finger marks on the table. I know The Man has been following me and I think he knows where I live. Doesn't support: I can't be certain that the mailbox wasn't open when I left the house. I was in a hurry to get to school and might not have noticed it or the finger marks. If he wanted me to know he'd been here, wouldn't he have left a note? I've never seen him anywhere near the house.
5. It's possible that my partner accidentally left the door open, even if he does usually close it. It's also highly possible that one of the bairns ran their fingers through the muck on the table. I could just be imagining things, like I did when I thought I saw him in the car.
6. Anxiety reduced to 2/5.

It was amazing, the difference it made. I had been completely convinced that The Man going through my mailbox was the only possible explanation. I had based my conviction on what I thought was intuition, but the exercise had made me realise there was something else going on here. I was in PTS mode and my brain was primed to see danger at every turn.

Psychologist and neuroscientist Professor Joel Pearson has spent several years studying the science of intuition.[1] His research has proven that humans are indeed able to make successful decisions without using rational thought, but there are some important caveats: intuition works best when we have some expertise in the area, and intuition can also be completely wrong. While our daily interactions with other people mean we all have a certain level of expertise in human behaviour and are able to pick up on valuable clues when someone's behaviour suggests danger, there are times when gut reactions can trick us. Pearson lists four situations where our intuition is likely to be less than reliable:

1. Moments of high emotion—if you've just fallen in love or had a massive argument with your partner, your heightened state of emotion is likely to mess with your intuitive signals. It's important to calm down and try to use logic before making any big decisions.
2. Predicting low-probability events—the idea that the plane you're about to board is going to crash is a powerful feeling that is likely to engage your amygdala, but it's not

intuition. It's very difficult for humans to predict low-probability events.

3. When your brain is engaged with primal impulses such as appetite, fear, lust and aggression—again, these are powerful emotions that can overwhelm the brain, but they're driven by evolutionary impulses, not intuitive understanding.

4. New environments—when we're in unfamiliar situations, it can often affect our unconscious signals and make intuition difficult to rely on.

Intuition can be a powerful tool when you need to react quickly, but that same fight-or-flight instinct can also become a trigger for unnecessary anxiety. This is where CBT comes in, where logic and cognitive evaluation can help us understand the situation more fully.

I was experiencing the stress of trauma, so my sympathetic nervous system was in overdrive and, however certain I was that I 'knew' what was going on, my 'intuition' couldn't be relied on to accurately predict or explain events. In going through the sheet, I was able to understand that the 'truth' I was telling myself was just something my brain had fabricated. On an immediate level, this was an enormous relief. There was still an undercurrent of anxiety, but I was no longer trapped inside that cubicle of horror and helplessness. It also demonstrated to me that changing our thinking, in all sorts of ways, is possible.

The malleability of the brain actually informs a lot of CBT practice, and much has been discovered and written about neuroplasticity in recent years. The brain's ability to rewire itself when connections are lost or broken is much greater than scientists previously realised. If one of the neural pathways in the brain is damaged, its function can usually be replicated by a different pathway. The brain can be encouraged to find this new pathway through sensory and motor stimulation. Stroke patients, for example, might participate in music therapy and virtual environment training to retrain their brains. Amazingly, mentally practising physical moves also helps to build new pathways for motor functions.[2]

Repetition is key here; once a neural pathway has been established, it needs to be used. And the more frequently it's used, the stronger it becomes. This is often likened to building a road or a bridge. If you wanted to get to the other side of a chasm, you might start by swinging across on a rope. Maybe you would attach a second rope to form a rudimentary bridge. If you travelled that route frequently, you would make the bridge stronger by adding some planks. As your crossings increased, you might turn it into a wooden bridge, maybe even a steel one with multiple lanes for all the traffic. Your bridge would become easier and quicker to cross. This is great news if you're retraining your brain after loss of function, but in certain situations it can have a negative impact.

Let's say, from a young age, you periodically hear women who are upset or angry being dismissed as hysterical.

Initially, your brain will throw a rope or two from 'angry woman' to 'hysteria'. But if the idea continues to be reinforced (you see distraught women in films being slapped in order to 'bring them to their senses', for example, or 'mad' wives in novels being locked away in attics), the bridge gets stronger. Eventually you see an angry woman and automatically think *hysterical*. And every time you think it, every time you say it, the bridge gets easier to cross. Maybe one day you yourself are described as hysterical. *Of course,* you think, *I'm voicing my anger, my distress, I must be hysterical.* You start to feel ridiculous every time you get angry or upset, so you shut your mouth around the noise of it, you freeze it in your throat, you push it back down to boil and bubble in your stomach, your organs, your joints, your cells.

Or let's say you're told that intuition is nonsense, something associated with the feminine, something to be scoffed at as unscientific and far inferior to those thought processes associated with the masculine: logic, evaluation, consideration. You start to override those gut feelings and early warning signs with phrases like *I'm being paranoid, I'm imagining things, I'm being ridiculous.*

Or let's say you're told that persistent pursuit is romantic, that continuing to badger an ex-partner when a relationship is over is an indication of deep love. Say you've been brought up with films and TV programs where a man doing his utmost to coerce a woman into a romantic engagement is seen as a sign of true love, where the man in a heterosexual relationship is EXPECTED to actively pursue a woman, while the woman must passively allow herself to be won over. It won't come as any surprise when you tell people you have a stalker and they say, *Are you sure you're not exaggerating? Maybe he just likes you.* It won't be unusual for you to say those same things to yourself.

These are just a few examples of the subtle mechanisms a misogynistic culture can use to ensure its survival, ways of justifying coercive behaviours and silencing those who might complain about them.

In her book *Trauma and Recovery*,[3] Judith Herman has a wonderful example of the patriarchal machine changing the truth in order to support itself. She describes Freud's work with women who had been sexually abused in their childhood by their fathers or other male relatives. After listening to woman after woman relate details of the abuse they had experienced, Freud developed his 'seduction theory', which proposed that early childhood sexual abuse could lead to neurosis. However, at some later date, Freud changed his mind. These women were not speaking of actual events, he claimed, but were in fact describing their own personal fantasies and desires. They WANTED these male authority figures to rape them, so they IMAGINED that they had been raped. From this, he developed his theory of psychosexual development. As Herman puts it, 'The dominant psychological theory of the next century was founded in the denial of women's reality.'

It was a denial that stuck. In his book *The Body Keeps the Score*, Bessel van der Kolk[4] mentions that the standard psychology textbook in the US in the 1980s claimed that incest was highly unusual and in fact only one in every million women were abused by family members. Even more alarmingly, the book stated that father–daughter 'incestuous activity diminishes the chance of psychosis and allows for a better adjustment to the external world'. Clearly, the survivors of incest were either not being listened to or not being believed.

Even more recently, Deborah Epstein and Lisa Goodman[5] have described how laws designed to protect women often fail, simply because the women's accounts of sexual harassment and abuse are not believed. By playing on negative cultural stereotypes of women and their motivations for seeking justice, legal gatekeepers can throw doubt on, or even completely dismiss, complainants' testimonies. Not only does this mean perpetrators of violent crimes may not be held to account, it deals a further blow to the already damaged confidence and well-being of survivors and makes it all the harder for them to heal.

Through my research, I began to understand the enormity of the patriarchal machine and the extent of my immersion in it. Over the years, my brain had accumulated ways of thinking about myself in relation to men that supported misogynistic culture. For example:

- My value as a person is based mostly on my appearance.

- I shouldn't cause offence if it's possible to avoid it by keeping my mouth shut.
- It's my job to ensure that people around me feel safe and comfortable.
- My own needs are less important than the needs and desires of others.
- If I attract unwanted male attention, it's probably my own fault for dressing inappropriately or being too friendly or otherwise giving out the 'wrong signals'.
- Any feelings of frustration, rage or powerlessness are best kept to myself. If I speak out, I will likely be seen as hysterical/insane/high maintenance and/or potentially put myself in danger.

Nobody had said any of this directly to me—I had imbibed these messages from noticing the roles women took on, from observing reactions to the behaviour of myself and other women, in real life, in newspapers, in films, in books and on television. The culture I was brought up in had built many steel bridges in my brain and I was using them to travel unwittingly into inhospitable, and sometimes down-right dangerous, territory.

In *The Gift of Fear*, de Becker[6] points out that before someone commits a violent crime on a stranger, they will generally go through a selection process. There are several ways of reducing your chances of being selected as a victim, and none of them depend on being polite or demure. In fact, quite the opposite. For example, if someone approaches you in a badly lit carpark and offers to help you load shopping into your car, you're probably best to say no thanks. If they carry on insisting, then you must forget about being polite. Instead, you must insist louder: I SAID NO! If someone tries to involve you in conversation and you feel a sense of apprehension, you should stop worrying about being rude. You should refuse to engage by ignoring them or walking away. You should never give in to someone just because they want you to. Those bridges in my brain, the ones that told me I needed to put others before myself, had the potential to put me in danger, especially when dealing with strangers.

CBT taught me that it's possible to dismantle those bridges and build new ones. It's possible to retrain your brain to think differently, to see an angry woman and say to yourself, *Quite right, she's probably got a lot to be angry about*, to look back at the teacher who screamed at you for writing your name on your jotter and wonder if she was actually screaming about her own lost opportunities, the fact that she had been looking after thirty-plus kids at once, all on her own, for years and years, with very little financial reward or recognition. The fact that she'd been looked over for promotion, time and time again, in favour of men, and she was fed up with being put down and disrespected and belittled and disempowered because she was a woman, and it was the seventies and she was just expected to put up with it. You can start to realise that things are bloody complicated, that we need both intuition AND logic to make sense of things. You can start to realise that change needs to happen on many different levels and that we can't do it on our own.

At a medical examination

In the nineties, when I go down to London to study for my BA, one of the subjects I choose is Education. I'm told I need to get a certificate of physical fitness before I can participate in this course. Nobody tells me why, and for some reason I don't ask. I suppose there's no one TO ask.

My partner at the time is also in London and he comes with me to the address I've been given. The examinations are taking place in a cavernous Victorian building somewhere in the heart of the city. I sit in the waiting room with several other young women and one or two men, all about to be examined for the same reason. The whole day has been set aside for this, with a constant stream of students coming and going between three or four doctors.

When it's my turn, I go into a room with high ceilings, tall, arched windows, a large wooden desk in the corner next to the window and a bed with a curtain around it in the opposite corner. The doctor is an older man, surely close to retirement if not already retired, perhaps just called in for these examinations when they need some extra hands for a routine job. He seems friendly and gentle, tells me to take a seat at the desk while he asks questions about my general health and writes down my answers. When he's done, he tells me to take a seat on the bed while he finishes off the forms. *I'll start by checking your lungs*, he says. *Could you undress, please. You can leave your underwear on.*

I'm a bit taken aback. I hadn't expected to have to undress and I feel embarrassed and vulnerable, sitting there in my bra and knickers. It doesn't seem quite right, but then I haven't been told what the examination entails. Maybe this is necessary.

When the doctor is ready, he comes over with his stethoscope and sits on the bed beside me. He apologises for his cold hands, the cold metal of the stethoscope. He places the stethoscope on various parts of my chest and asks me to breathe slowly in and out. His own breath seems quick and laboured and his hands shake as he moves the stethoscope from the top of one breast to the other and back again. Then he asks me to turn around so he can listen on my back. *I just need to undo your bra strap so I can listen here,* he says. He fumbles with it. *I'm sorry, I'm not very good at this.* He gives a little laugh. *My wife always complains about that.*

It's there again, that feeling that something isn't quite right. Does he really need to undo my bra? The way he's shaking, the laboured breath, is it just his age, or is he excited, turned on? I'm confused and upset. All I know is that I don't like what's being done to me, but it doesn't feel like there's anything I can do about it. He's a doctor. He's examining me. He hasn't done anything I can pinpoint as definitely wrong.

Finally, he asks me to stand up so he can check my posture. He has me face the window, and I stand looking out across the grey London rooftops, in my bra and knickers, while he crouches on the floor behind me with a small torch. He moves my legs apart and repositions my feet and then spends maybe five minutes on the floor 'checking my posture'. I have no idea what he's doing, but he's very close. I can feel his breath on the back of my thighs. I want to burst into tears. I know that something odd is happening and I have the feeling I'm being violated and yet what would I tell people if they asked? *He was looking at my legs for too long? He was breathing too heavily?* It doesn't feel like enough.

Eventually the doctor tells me to get dressed and he goes back to his desk to finish the paperwork. He chats away, friendly and conversational, until I start to wonder if I've imagined the impropriety. *I'm just a harmless old doctor,* he seems to be saying to me. *Nothing to worry about here.*

I go back to the waiting room and find my partner. *Are you okay?* he asks when he sees my face. I shake my head and hurry him down the stairs. As soon as we get outside, I burst into tears. *What's wrong?* he asks. *What happened?*

I don't know, I say, *it was just weird.* I try to explain the doctor's shaking hands, undoing my bra strap, his breath on the back of my legs.

He shrugs. *I don't get it,* he says. *Was it because he was old that you didn't like it? He didn't touch you anywhere, did he?*

No, I said, *he didn't touch me.* I feel stupid, like I'm over-reacting. I don't mention it again, not to anyone.

———

My middle-aged self sees it differently: a man getting his jollies examining young women, pushing it as far as he can without doing anything he can be struck off for, probably telling himself he isn't doing anything wrong. My middle-aged self is furious that the college was sending young girls to him to be examined. That stream of young women he could have disrobing in front of him, his ability to ever-so-subtly manipulate them. I'm furious that there weren't stronger controls over who was chosen for this job. At the very least it should have been a female doctor that examined the women. I still don't know why it was even a requirement to have a physical examination or why there was no explanation, in advance, of what to expect. Mostly I'm angry at myself for not speaking out and at the culture that taught me to say nothing about abuse of power.

because the patriarchal system depends on everyone obeying those in authority, because, historically, those in authority have mostly been men, because words like harridan, harpy, ball-breaker, witch, battle-axe, dragon, Karen, nag are used to shame women and discourage them from complaining, because men are significantly more likely than women to believe gender-based inequality is no longer a problem in Australia,[7] because if you don't experience something, it's easier to believe it doesn't exist, because a 2018 survey by the SA Law Society reported a 'concerning' level of harassment in the legal workplace, because the report also found that most victims were women in junior roles and that harassment often occurred where there was a power imbalance between victim and perpetrator,[8] because a PRESIDENT of the UNITED STATES has physically and verbally assaulted women, because he has said about the women who accuse him of assault that they're lying, not because he would never do such a thing, but because 'She's not my type', because 'Look at her, I don't think so', because 'Believe me, she would not be my first choice',[9] because 'When you're a star, they let you do it . . . Grab 'em by the pussy. You can do anything',[10] because this says everything there is to say about his attitude to women (entitlement, disrespect, woman as object), because THIS DID NOT STOP HIM BEING VOTED IN AS PRESIDENT, because Harvey Weinstein, because Jeffrey Epstein, because Tony Abbott, because 'ditch the witch', because Alan Jones, because 'shove a sock down her throat', because gendered violence, because sexual harassment, because rape, because stalking, because women still have a lot to complain about and the system is still trying to silence them

CHAPTER 10

The search for security.
The impact of The Man
on my family life

After I discovered I was being followed, there were months and months of crazy days when my mind raced around like a cartoon roadrunner, beep-beeping at every passing shadow. I was exhausted, mentally and physically. Much as I tried to keep my anxiety bundled up in the same black cloth I kept my anger in, bits of it would escape from the folds and flit around our home. Its dark energy buzzed in every room, batted wildly against windows looking for a way out.

There were things I thought my family should know. Since I was the only one who had actually seen and spoken to The Man, I felt like I was the authority, the one who KNEW (from the tight shape his mouth made, from the cave in his voice, from the ice in his eyes) that a ghastly river of violent intent ran through everything he said and did. No one else was getting this, and I felt it was imperative, for their safety, that they did.

I tried to keep it casual, but how do you casually inform your children that their mother is being followed by a man with a ghastly river inside him and that he might come after them too? There's no way to make that sound anything other than terrifying.

In many ways that was the worst thing about that period of my life, the impact it had on my children. I didn't know how to protect them from him and protect them from me at the same time. My son I was less anxious about; I dropped him off at primary school, I took him to sports events or to friends' houses, and I picked him up later. He was never wandering around on his own. But the two older children had to travel across the city on public transport to get to and from school. The eldest was in her final year—her start and finish times were different—so the two of them rarely travelled together.

I told them both about The Man. I said, *It's probably okay but, just in case, watch out for anyone following you. Whatever anyone says, don't go away anywhere with them if you don't know them.* I made them both carry rape alarms, attached to their key rings. I told them to hold their keys in their hands when they were walking alone in the street.

My eldest (confident, resilient, about to fly off to university) would roll her eyes and shake her head. *Whatever, Mum ...* It's reassuring now to think that maybe she didn't take any of it too seriously, protected by that late-teen certainty that nothing can harm you and your parents are clueless idiots. But my middle child was younger, more vulnerable.

In the early days, when my habitual mental state was *anxiety 4/5*, I walked to the train station with my middle child if they were going to school alone, and I waited with them till their train arrived, my eyes flicking over the other passengers on the platform, the faces in the carriage they got into, scanning for predators like a nervous meerkat. I got them to text me when they arrived at school and when they were on their way back, so I knew when to expect them. If they were even slightly late, I would leave the house and go and stand at the end of our street, waiting till I saw them in the distance, bare legs pale beneath their school skirt, schoolbag like a giant tortoiseshell on their back, ambling home with earbud wires dangling round their face. I tried to disappear back to the house before they noticed me teetering on the edge of the pavement, a half-crazed nutter of a mother, always on the brink of crying out *Wolf*.

My partner was very patient with all this. When I said, *We've got to move back to Scotland, it's not safe here anymore*, he said, *Well, that's certainly possible, but let's have a think about how we can do it*. When I said, *The Man might be watching the house, he might try and break in, we need to get a security system*, he said, *Okay, let's get someone to come and have a look and give us a price for one*. I know that as well as being anxious about the situation, he must have been anxious about the effect it was having on me, but he was always calm and considerate. He didn't make fun of me or call me a nutter; he took my concerns seriously. I doubt whether he would actually have gone through with the enormous upheaval of moving back to Scotland, but he was prepared to talk through the idea, trusting, I imagine, that I would eventually come to my senses.

Not long after the park incident, we went with the bairns to JB Hi-Fi so we could look at home security systems. While we poked around among the different cameras, the bairns went off to look at phones. In the relatively private corridor between two floor-to-ceiling displays, my partner and I discussed our options. He wanted to wait for a bit before we committed to a system. He wanted to do some more research, maybe have someone come round to the house and give us advice. I wanted security NOW and had decided that a camera (or two, or three) outside the house might make me feel safer inside. I had conveniently forgotten that the rattling stones of panic were inside me. Pouring over camera footage to see if The Man ever appeared outside the house was not going to settle them. Still, I was wild with anxiety and just wanted something, anything, that would stop my brain from shrieking. In my desperation, I forgot all about my decision not to let the crazy out.

I don't think I can go another week like this, I said to my partner. *You don't understand what it's like. I'm scared to be in the house in case he's outside, getting ready to smash his way in, and I'm scared to be outside, in case he's waiting for me, waiting for the opportunity to bundle me into the back of a van. Who knows what he's capable of? He could be completely psychotic and he could be anywhere. He could be here right now, watching us.*

My partner laid a hand on my arm as if to quieten me. His face was deadly serious. He gave a quick jerk of his head towards the end of the corridor we were standing in, his eyes flashing alarm. I turned slowly round, expecting to see The Man standing there, staring at us.

It wasn't The Man, it was our children.

I was horrified. I wanted to swallow everything I'd said. I wanted to run to them, put my arms around them, tell them everything would be okay. But it was too late. Once again, the terror I tried to keep bundled inside me had slipped out and made itself known.

In another attempt to protect myself and the two eldest, I enrolled us all in Wing Tsun classes, which I chose because the focus was on self-defence rather than martial art. Once a week we went along to a Scout hall where we learnt how to 'absorb the strength of our attacker and redirect it back towards them'. We always opened with the same routine, a slightly aggressive version of Tai Chi, involving slo-mo punches, twists and kicks. I loved the rhythm and rep-etition, the balletic grace of it. My mind relaxed easily into the action and forgot everything else.

It was a small class, usually around eight of us in total. All the others were men who had been doing Wing Tsun for some time. They were very welcoming, happy to practise with us, and it felt good to inch towards them, punching into their body shields while they moved back, shouting, *Good! Keep going! Punch harder!*

After a few months we stopped the classes. Not because they weren't enjoyable (although the bairns did say they found it a bit weird, being so much younger than everyone else) but because, inevitably, the focus was on the many ways a man might try to physically overcome you. *If a man is following you in the street . . . If a man comes up to you in a bar . . .*

If a man tries to grab you from behind/cover your mouth/ touch you inappropriately . . . I worried about what it was teaching my children about men and the world in general. I didn't want them to grow up fearful. And yet, spoken or unspoken, my own frenetic fear buzzed around them daily.

One day, I was up in the Adelaide Hills where I was doing some interior design for a client. While I was there, my phone ran out of charge. I didn't notice until I looked at the clock and realised the alarm, set for the train that would get me back to Adelaide in time to pick up my son from school, hadn't gone off. I raced down to the Blackwood station, but it was too late: I'd missed it. I had a half-hour wait for the next train, but I'd cycled to the Adelaide station that morning and left my bike locked up there. I figured if I just cycled like a spider on caffeine, I could get from the station to my son's school and only be twenty minutes late.

I counted down the stations on the way back. Blackwood, Coromandel, Eden Hills, Lynton. Twenty minutes. Was that too late? My son always played for a bit with friends after school, maybe he wouldn't even notice I wasn't there. But what if The Man turned up? What if he saw that I wasn't there and decided to take advantage of the opportunity, tell my son some story about me: an accident, a kidnapping, an alien abduction? When the train pulled into Adelaide station, I practically commando-rolled through the doors and onto the platform. I sprinted for the bike rack, unlocked my bike and wheeled it to the exit, ticket in hand, ready to open the electronic gate. There were two members of staff on duty, a young woman and a middle-aged man. I pressed my ticket to the machine and started to walk through when the man stopped me.

Just a minute, he said. *It's after three o'clock. Where's the ticket for your bike?*

Oh, I didn't take my bike on the train, I said. *I cycled to the station this morning and left it in the lock-up while I went to Blackwood.*

It's after three, he said. *Bikes need tickets after three.*

What, even if I haven't taken it on the train? I asked. *Do I need to pay to lock it up here?*

How do I know that you locked it up? he said.

I looked at him, baffled. *Er . . . because I'm telling you?*

How do I know you're telling the truth?

I don't suppose you do, I said. *I suppose you just have to take my word for it.* I grinned hopefully at him.

He just stood there looking at me, shaking his head, tutting as if I was a naughty child.

I'm actually late to pick my son up from school, I explained. *Can you just tell me what you want me to do? Are you saying I have to go and buy a ticket for my bike if I want to take it out of the station?* I glanced back at the information desk where you could buy tickets. There was a queue of four or five people and it didn't seem to be moving particularly fast.

That's between you and your conscience, he said.

Well, my conscience is clear, I said. *I know I haven't had my bike on the train, so does that mean I can go through the gate?*

He shook his head sadly. *The problem is I don't know if you've had your bike on the train.*

I looked around, wondering if I'd somehow wandered onto the film set of a Kafka novel. The young woman leaned forward, her face creased with embarrassment. *Look, I think you're just going to have to buy a ticket,* she said. *Sorry.*

I hurried back to the information desk, wheeling my bike with me, hopped about in the queue while several people took Far Longer Than Necessary to get the information they needed, bought my ticket and returned to the gate. By this time, I was seething. Steam was practically blasting from my nostrils and tiny daggers had popped out of my eyes. I was so overcome with anxiety, I had no time to think of things from the man's point of view. As far as I was concerned, he was a petty jobsworth who was prepared to put bureaucracy before my son's safety. I stopped in front of him. *Could you tell me your name, please?* I asked.

He smiled, slid his hands into his trouser pockets. I could see the corner of the name tag that was pinned to his jumper sticking out from under the edge of his jacket, but the writing was hidden. *You don't need to know my name,* he said, as if he was Obi-Wan Kenobi.

If you're not going to tell me your name, I'd like to speak to whoever's in charge, I replied.

I'm in charge here, he said. *You don't need to speak to anyone else.*

Dear god, did he actually think he had The Force? I could feel large, pus-filled boils of anger popping out all over my skin, but I was late enough as it was. I really didn't have time for this. I pressed the bike ticket onto the electronic pad and wheeled my bike through, turning back to point the daggers in my eyes directly at the man. Then I cycled off, legs going like veritable pistons.

When I arrived at the school, it was almost forty minutes since the bell had gone. The playground was empty. I walked round the outside of the school, calling my son's name. Nothing. *Nothingnothingnothingnothing.* I tried his class-room, but there was no one there and his bag was gone from its peg. Close to hyperventilating, I went to the front office to ask if anyone knew where he was. Nobody did.

Maybe someone gave him a lift home, Eileen, the office manager, suggested. *Has nobody phoned you?*

My battery's dead, I said. *I don't suppose you have a charger here.*

They didn't. I cycled home, pistons on full power, whispering to myself, *Please let him be there, please let him be there*, over and over. The street was empty. No car parked outside the house, no one waiting at the front door. I think I might have started crying. I fumbled the key into the lock, rushed inside, plugged my phone in and sat hunched over it, waiting for the Shining White Apple of Salvation to appear.

After about three decades, the phone finally sprang to life. Two missed calls and a voicemail from Lucy, the mother of one of my son's friends. *Hope everything's okay. I didn't want to leave your son at the school on his own, so I've just taken him back to ours. He's welcome to stay for dinner if that's okay with you, but let me know if you want me to run him home.*

I cried some more, tears of relief this time. *Thankgodthankgodthankgod.*

I phoned Lucy. *I'm SO sorry*, I said, *I was up in the hills and didn't realise my phone had died. I couldn't even phone the school to let them know I'd be late.*

Not a problem at all, she replied. She apologised for taking him away rather than waiting for me at the school. *I just thought he was getting a bit anxious and I wanted to take his mind off it*, she said. *He seemed really worried about you. He said a man had been following you.*

Even now, my heart crumbles a bit round the edges when I think of that wee boy, looking round for his mum, scared that someone has hurt her or taken her away. I start blaming myself all over again. *Could I not have kept all that inside? Did I really have to involve the bairns, frighten them with my over-the-top warnings, my out-of-proportion fear?* I can't bear to think about what it must have done to them.

In a club

I'm almost eight months pregnant with my first child and I'm living in Edinburgh. My friend's thirtieth birthday is coming up and she's organised a night out at Pure, a club that we're deeply fond of and go to regularly. Or, in my case, used to go to. I haven't been to any club since I found out I was pregnant, and I'm not sure it's the right thing to do. Do pregnant women go clubbing? I can't remember ever seeing any. On the other hand, I can't think of any reason that a pregnant woman shouldn't go to a club. It's not like I'll be drinking or taking drugs, just dancing. I miss those happy, heady nights, lost in the throb of sound and light, sharing wild grins with those who danced around me, and I want to celebrate my friend's birthday with her. But social convention tells me that pregnant women stay at home of an evening, pouring over parenthood manuals or knitting bootees and bonnets for their soon-to-arrive babies. Am I already a 'bad mother' for even considering going to a place like Pure?

Pure takes place in The Venue, which, contrary to the name of the club, is probably the grimiest dive in Edinburgh. Everything has a knocked-about look. Paint is peeling, doors are scuffed, and the toilets regularly flood to the point where you have to swish ankle deep through water if you want to use them. Often people just go outside. What isn't contrary is the vibe. Pure is all about the music and the community. No swank or glitter, no podiums or cages, just a mass of bonded dancers, embedded in the sounds, meshed in the down and dirty of the music's grass roots. The grime is irrelevant when resident DJs Twitch and Brainstorm are on the decks, playing tracks that slip from Belgian rave into deep house into soul techno into tribal rhythms. The musical phrases shift over each other, changing, building momentum, sliding back to transcendental waves, carrying the crowd on a tide of pure joy. Sometimes the DJs surprise us with incongruous tunes like AC/DC's 'The Ace of Spades', which triggers an explosion of headbanging and helpless laughter, or Donna Summer's 'I Feel Love', which melts everyone into an all-encompassing embrace. Often the room is so full of dry ice that it feels celestial, like everyone else has disappeared and you're dancing alone inside a cloud and could carry on dancing forever. If you aren't already soaked in sweat by the end of the night, you only have to lean against the river of condensation running down the walls to absorb the accumulated sweat of everyone else in the club. We don't mind the grunge. We're there to be part of Pure's extended family, a great and glorious tribe of people who look out for one another, whose smiles break through the clouds and fill you with a sense of belonging. It's this that makes me decide it'll be okay, that I'll be safe, even with a wee baby kicking inside me.

My partner and I are living in a flat at the top of Leith Walk, easy walking distance to Pure. We've agreed to meet the others in The Basement Bar, so, rugged up with jumpers, coats, hats and scarves, we skite along the icy November pavements to Broughton Street.

There's quite a crowd, almost twenty of us, standing at the bar or squeezed in round a table, sitting on each other's knees or leaning in, arms round shoulders. Shots are knocked back and Es passed round and the air above us fills with the buzz and twinkle of pre-club excitement. I stand on the fringes of the group, sooking orange juice from a schooner, one hand resting on my rounded belly.

Eventually we all tumble along the road to the club, singing and waving to other groups of people headed in the same direction. Some are running and sliding down the hill in long, graceful glides. I want to join in, but the bump I carry in front of me reminds me I can't risk falling. I hobble along, taking short, careful steps across the frosty ground, hanging onto my partner's arm.

We enter the club via the basement, where the chill-out room is. Bill's on the decks. He's friendly with some of our crowd and often DJs at the after-parties we go to. I feel like I'm being welcomed home as the white feathers of Björk's 'Venus as a Boy' flutter against my ears. I spot someone I know, sitting cross-legged in a corner with a group of friends, eyes closed, nodding along to Björk while her thumbs spin round a fat cone. I touch my partner's arm. *I'm just going to go and speak to Kate*, I say. *I'll come upstairs and find you in a bit.*

Are you sure? he asks. *You don't want me to wait here with you?*

No, I'll be fine, I say. *You go up with the others.*

Kate's face opens in amazement when she sees me. *Look at you!* she says, standing up to give me a hug. *I haven't seen you for ages. How are you? When are you due? Come and sit down.*

I sit and chat for a bit, then go up to the bar to get myself a bottle of water. I'm waiting for the bartender to finish serving and have half-turned to watch the small crowd of dancers when I see someone coming towards me. He's short and stocky with a Madchester haircut and a Hearts football top. His eyes are fixed on me, but he isn't anyone I know. He doesn't look like a Pure regular, either. His face is bitten with anger.

What the fuck do you think you're doing here? he says when he gets closer. *You've no business being in here, you slutty cow.* He has the teeth-gritty, wide-eyed look of a coke-head, so I figure he's just overdone it and is freaking out.

It's okay, mate, I say to him, *I think you're maybe mistaking me for someone else. I honestly don't know who you are.*

Don't give me that shite, he says, his voice getting louder. He pushes his shoulders towards me, neck muscles like bat wings, hands screwed into fists. *You better get the fuck out of here or I'm going to beat the crap out of you. GET FUCKING HOME, RIGHT NOW!*

A few people at the bar turn to look at him, and then at me, their expressions like question marks. This isn't normal Pure behaviour. A sense of shame creeps in around my edges. Maybe they think Madchester and I are together. In any case, I can tell there isn't going to be any reasoning with him, so

I walk, as nonchalantly as I can, away from the bar, praying he won't follow me. I'm very conscious of my vulnerability, the vulnerability of the bump I'm carrying. Kate waves me over as I go past, but I point upstairs and keep moving.

Entering the main part of the club is like passing through a portal. I'm engulfed in the vortex of sound, bass throbbing in my torso. Pulsing strobe lights give everyone the jerky movements of an early motion picture, and scanning the sea of bobbing heads is like scrolling through old film footage. Eventually I locate my partner and make my way through ice cloud and space lights to find him. He grins when he sees me and throws an arm round my waist, drawing me into the rhythm of his dance. For a moment it feels good to enter the wilds of the music, but I can't forget the threat of the man downstairs.

Are you okay? my partner says into my ear. I tell him what happened. *Really?* he says. *In Pure? Even worse, in The Cooler! Totally ruining the vibe. Did he follow you?*

No, I say, *he was watching me when I went out the door, but he didn't come after me. Maybe he thought I was leaving.*

Let's just stay here, says my partner. *Hopefully he'll forget about you.*

He doesn't. Half an hour or so later, he reappears, muscling his way through the dry ice like a storm cloud headed in my direction. *I THOUGHT I TOLD YOU TO LEAVE,* he yells above the music, his bottom teeth sliding maniacally to and fro across the top ones. *YOU BETTER FUCKING PAY ATTENTION, I'VE JUST ABOUT HAD IT WITH YOU!*

Mate, you need to chill out, says my partner, stepping between us. *She's here with me. She doesn't know you.*

SHE'S NO BUSINESS BEING HERE IN HER CONDITION, yells Madchester. *SHE NEEDS TO BE AT HOME! GET HER FUCKING HOME!*

It suddenly dawns on me that this is about me being pregnant. Although he's clearly off his nut on something, Madchester hasn't mistaken me for someone else; he's mistaken himself for the caretaker of my pregnant body. As rage pops in his bulging veins, all kinds of possibly about-to-occur violence play rapidly through my head like the gory trailer of a horror movie. But other people have also noticed what's going on. We're gradually being surrounded by what you might call Concerned Onlookers. One tall guy with dreads claps a hand on Madchester's shoulder.

Brother, he says, *how are we doing here? Is everything okay?*

Look at the state of her, says Madchester through gritted teeth. *She shouldn't be here. So fucking irresponsible. Really fucking ANNOYS ME!* His face collapses into menace and he drops into a squat, roaring like a beast of the moors, fists balled and quivering.

The guy with dreads crouches down beside him. I can't hear what's being said, but eventually the two of them stand up and make their way back through the crowd in the direction of the bar. The Concerned Onlookers move in around us. We don't really know any of them, though some are familiar faces, Pure regulars.

Are you okay?

Fuck, that was a bit intense!

What was UP with that guy?

Not long after, the guy with the dreads comes back. *He's gone now*, he says. *I let the bouncers know not to let him back in.*

I'm amazed that he's persuaded Madchester to leave. *Thank you so much*, I say. We hug. My partner shakes his hand.

Good job, mate, says someone else.

We all chat for a while, raising our voices above the sounds, but eventually we knit ourselves back into the music, letting it fill us until we become something much bigger and smaller than everything that just happened.

because the idea that a man should take care of a woman is still common, because although it has tones of chivalry and gallantry, it also suggests patronisation and control, because it is rooted in Victorian notions of women as 'the weaker sex', women and men operating in 'separate spheres', men out in public and women at home, where they won't be exposed to immorality, men as financial providers and protectors, women as intellectually immature, childlike in their thinking,[1] because women who railed against this lifestyle were given 'Dr Mitchell's Rest Cure for nervous women', which involved months of enforced bed rest, with no writing or reading, because Mitchell claimed that 'no group of men so truly interprets, comprehends and sympathizes with women, as do physicians, who know how near to disorder and how close to misfortune she is brought by the very peculiarities of her nature',[2] because Charlotte Perkins Gilman's short story 'The yellow wallpaper'[3] tells how the 'Rest Cure' nearly drove her insane, because although these ideas seem ridiculous today, some of the attitudes still persist, because men are still asking women to let them look after us and to be appreciative when they do, because it makes them feel like our protectors, because it makes them feel like they have the power to please us[4]

CHAPTER 11

Things I do to stay sane

When I looked into ways of coping with stress, I found out it was very common for people exposed to trauma to self-medicate, often by using alcohol or cannabis. Both substances, in low doses, can make you feel more sociable and cheery, give you a sense of bonhomie and alleviate anxiety. If you're used to dealing with your problems by yourself, rather than seeking help, alcohol or cannabis might seem like a good solution.

For some people, trauma starts in childhood, but I was lucky. Although we never had much money, we were well fed and appropriately clothed, and I had loving, supportive parents who were always around for me. I was encouraged to go to university—at that time grants were available for students whose families couldn't afford the fees. I don't remember therapy ever being spoken about when I was growing up, but as an adult I knew it was a valid way of dealing with problems. I didn't seek counselling after being raped or after a violent relationship, but I had a good network of supportive family and friends who helped me through those difficult times. I don't know why my experience with The Man caused me so much more distress, but I could see I wasn't coping. I knew I needed help, and I was able to access it. I know it's not that easy for everyone.

And for some reason, I didn't turn to alcohol, though I'd always been someone who enjoyed a drink. In fact, I became scared of alcohol. I knew a few glasses of wine might relax me and send me off to sleep but they would also have me waking at three in the morning, on my own in the dark and filled with demon thoughts. Afraid of the places my alcohol-soaked brain might take me, I stopped drinking altogether.

I also stopped watching crime shows. The stories of psychopaths—serial killers, people traffickers, rapists, child abusers—would start the stones rattling inside me. So many stories of people being mutilated, murdered, psychologically damaged, shows I had once watched for entertainment. Fear is not so thrilling when it's real. Instead, I turned to the benign calm of wildlife and gardening programs, or the twee banality of family dramas I would never normally have had time for: *Doc Martin, Call the Midwife, The Middle*. The gentle humour and simple, easy-going plot lines were what my stressed-out brain craved.

But probably what was most important was spending time with friends, for two reasons. Firstly, I could talk about my experience of being stalked and, for the most part, be listened to sympathetically, have my fears taken seriously. Secondly, I could NOT talk about being stalked. I could forget about it altogether, wrap myself in the warm, safe blanket of friendship, share stories and laugh or commiserate. Although some friends had been baffled by the extent of my fearful reaction to seemingly innocuous incidents, their responses had been genuine efforts to reassure me, rather than deride me for my paranoia. I marvelled at how lucky I was to know so many caring, supportive people who were pleased to help in any way they could. And I realised something important: the reason I had such strong bonds with my friends was partly because of my tendency to be open and honest about who I was. It wasn't such a bad thing, after all. It might have made me an easy stalking target, but over the course of my life it had also brought me many wonderful relationships. I could stop blaming myself for being too naïve.

In fact, scientific research has consistently shown that having strong social support networks reduces psychological stress when bad things happen. It's known as the buffering effect. Keen to work out the reasons for this effect, Erica Hornstein and Naomi Eisenberger devised a test that would show whether or not social support prevented people from becoming fearful.[1] Participants in the test were shown images of a neutral object (a clock or a stool), one paired with the image of someone the participant had named as a strong support figure and the other paired with a similar-looking stranger. The images were displayed six times and the participants simultaneously given a mild electric shock.

By tracking brain activity, the researchers could see that participants began to respond fearfully to the object paired with a stranger but not to the object paired with their support figure. What's more, participants were later shown images of the clock and stool on their own (without an electric shock or the image of a person). They still responded with mild fear to the image that had been paired with a stranger, but no fear when shown the image that had been paired with their social support figure.

The research paper concluded that social support can protect us from life's stresses, and that even the presence of a social support reminder is powerful enough to reduce our reactions to threat. It can therefore be assumed that if you have stronger social ties you'll have fewer fear associations, and therefore less stress as you interact with the world. This explains previous research showing that people who have lots of good-quality friendships have better physical and mental health, not only being less susceptible to colds and coughs but also having a decreased risk of disease and premature death. Friends can literally save your life!

Getting married

I'm twenty-two and I have a job as a youth worker in a community centre in Wester Hailes, a housing scheme in Edinburgh. One of my colleagues, Graham, is a drummer in a band. He mentions they have a gig in one of the pubs in the Cowgate and asks if I want to go along.

The pub is a bit of a dive, the sort of place where your feet stick to the floor from all the spilt beer and you can smell the men's loos if you stand at the wrong end of the bar. But there's a big room through the back where bands play, sometimes really good bands. Once, by accident, I saw The Clash there. They were huge at the time, but for some reason they'd decided to travel by foot around Britain, busking in the streets and playing the occasional impromptu, unadvertised gig in a bar. I just happened to be there at the right time.

Graham's band isn't The Clash, but they're good. The lead singer looks (and sings) like Ian McCulloch from Echo and the Bunnymen, leaning into the mic, eyes closed, intense and moody. The bass guitarist turns out to be a girl I went to school with. Her fluid basslines hold the music perfectly, but for the entire performance she sits on a stool facing the back of the stage so all the audience see is her long blonde hair and the dark hunch of her shoulders. I think this is insanely cool. *It's not about how I look,* she seems to be saying, *it's about the music. Just listen.*

The lead guitarist is the one who captures most of my attention. Like the lead singer, he seems intensely serious, completely absorbed in the music. He looks down at his guitar, his blond curls flopping forward into his face, lips pouting in concentration, long fingers rippling across the strings. Mostly it's his eyes. Sharp blue with dark lashes. He looks up from his guitar only once, and when he does his eyes look straight into mine.

After the gig I help the band pack up and then we sit down for a drink. The guitarist (whose name is Alex) sits across the table from me, speaking to the bass player (Shona). I feel self-consciously uncool, my clothes not understated enough, my hair too frizz-ended and indefinite. I'm not surprised that neither Alex nor Shona seem to notice me. I think of saying to Shona, *Hey, didn't we go to the same school?* but I don't have the nerve to speak to either of them. They seem to come from a different world, one where nobody talks about school or breakfast or work or anything mundane. They're so deep in conversation that I start thinking they must be together, but when I get chatting to Graham about the gig, he mentions that Shona is in a relationship with the lead singer, Ewan, who has been absent since the gig finished. Alex is single! Quick fizz of excitement. Adrenaline pump. Heart thump. Then an exhale. It doesn't make any difference one way or the other, Alex is hardly going to be interested in ME.

But when Shona gets up to go to the bar, and Graham goes off to the loo, and it's just me and Alex at the table, he swivels round in his chair to face me. Damn, his eyes are blue! He looks at me for what feels like ages before he speaks. *So,* he says, *you're Graham's friend.*

I look down at my dishevelled self, tatty jeans, bobbled jumper. *Sure,* I say, *or colleague or whatever. We work together, but I mostly do youth work with the younger ones, after-school club, that sort of thing, and Graham works with the older bairns. Sometimes we do youth club together, or the discos, they usually need a lot of staff for the discos.*

I carry on, feeling like I'm havering, too many unnecessary details about my boring job, but when I look up he's smiling at me and I get a rush of something like fire zipping through me. We carry on talking and I find out he's not from another world at all, we actually have a lot in common, including living in flats in Haymarket that are owned by the same landlord.

We should share a taxi later, he says, and my heart gives another thump.

The taxi ends up being sooner rather than later. Graham comes back from the loo and tells us that Shona and Ewan are arguing at the bar. Ewan has sneaked off somewhere and come back pissed and now he's asking Shona to buy him a pint and she's refusing because he's pissed already and owes her from last week.

They'll be at it all night, says Graham. *Do yous fancy going somewhere else?*

We could just go back to mine, says Alex. *I've a bottle of vodka back there.*

Even this sounds cool. A bottle of vodka! Nobody I know keeps bottles of vodka in their flats. We're all too skint. Carryouts are bought for parties and drunk immediately, usually cheap wine and cans of Tennants or McEwans. Vodka, bought for nothing in particular, seems like a real luxury. I'm imagining a glass cabinet with glittering bottles of spirits, rows of cocktail glasses, maybe a jar of maraschino cherries.

We grab a taxi in the street and head towards Haymarket. Alex sits in the middle and I sit next to him. His thigh presses against mine. I'm so conscious of the heat through my jeans that I'm finding it difficult to concentrate on what's being said. At one point Alex turns to say something to me and rests his hand on my knee. He leaves it there for the rest of the journey.

When we pull up at Haymarket, Graham says he's changed his mind, he's going to take the taxi on to Wester Hailes. He needs to be up early tomorrow to go and get his drum kit from the pub.

Great gig, man, says Alex as we both jump out. *Great drumming.*

Graham waves through the back window as the taxi pulls away.

Alex lives in a tenement block on Dalry Road. He opens the stair door with a key and I follow him into the cool, echoey space of the communal stair. He turns back to look at me. The dusky light. His blue eyes. His lips. I smile at him and he rests his guitar against the wall and reaches out his hand and

I take it and he pulls me towards him and we kiss. It's a great kiss, gentle and passionate at the same time, his hand in the small of my back, running down to the back of my thigh and back up again. He stops for a minute, looks at me, grinning, then kisses me again.

Come on, he says, picking up his guitar and pulling me towards the stair.

There's no cocktail cabinet in Alex's room, and definitely no maraschino cherries. His room is bare and unadorned: just a double bed, a wardrobe, a chest of drawers. The bottle of vodka is on top of the chest of drawers. It's about three-quarters full, blue label, a brand I don't recognise. We sit on the bed together and we kiss a bit more, and then Alex goes to get some glasses. *Sorry, there're no mixers left*, he says when he arrives back. *Do you mind it straight?*

I've never had straight vodka before but I feel like I don't mind anything. I don't even mind drinking it out of a Hearts of Midlothian Football Club mug. I take tiny sips and the liquid fire of it burns all the way down. We drink and we talk and we kiss and then we get into bed together.

It's a bit of a whirlwind romance, accelerated by two things. The first is, a couple of weeks after we've started going out, our landlord gets busted for not paying taxes and has to sell off all his properties. We're both given a month's notice and we decide to look for a place together. It turns out Graham and Ewan are also looking for a place, so we all move into an enormous Georgian flat in Coates Gardens. Alex and I have the first-floor bedroom, Ewan and Graham are upstairs. The huge sitting room with marble fireplace and two bay windows is set up as the band practice room: mic stands, guitar stands, amps, Graham's drum kit. We all go off to our jobs during the day and at night we hang out in the practice room and play music and chat. Sometimes one of us cooks a meal and we sit with it on our knees, eating and playing and talking. Sometimes Shona joins us. Sometimes there are a few cans of beer going around, but not always. Sometimes I notice that Ewan seems a bit more pissed than I would expect him to be after a couple of cans. Alex never seems pissed, or not THAT pissed. Occasionally, he drifts off into creative mode, sitting picking out a melody on his guitar, stopping to scribble down dreamy, melancholic lyrics. He writes a couple of songs for me. They're so beautiful they make me want to cry. It feels like there's something very pure and astonishing between us. The way he looks at me when we're making love, the way he stops me and kisses me if we happen to pass each other when we're out somewhere, then walks away, leaving me breathless, longing to run after him. I'm madly in love with him, deliriously happy, except when I start to think he might leave me.

There's no real reason for me to think this. Yes, he sometimes comes home late from his work in the riding stables, after going to the pub with his workmates. Yes, he occasionally seems sullen and distant, doesn't want to talk, just sits morosely picking away at his guitar. But there's nothing wrong with going for a spontaneous drink with his mates, nothing wrong with occasionally feeling a bit down. For the most part he's loving and considerate. There's really nothing to worry about, but this is the intense, obsessive stage of early love and I'm a Hills Hoist of spinning emotions—euphoric when I think my passion is reciprocated, devastated when I feel there's a chance it might not be.

Before I met Alex, I had been accepted onto a BA course in London, and this is the second thing that accelerates the relationship. I'm going to be moving to London in a couple of months. We talk about it one night, lying on our backs in the double bed, staring up at the elaborate ceiling rose around the single bare bulb.

You'll probably forget all about me when you go to London, Alex says. *You'll meet someone else.*

I roll over to face him. *No, I won't,* I say. *Of course I won't. You'll probably forget about ME.*

Alex turns to face me. He puts his hand on my hip. *We could always get married,* he says.

I burst out laughing, but stop when I see his face. There's something in his eyes. He looks hurt. *You're kidding, aren't you?* I say.

No, he replies. *I really do want to marry you. I never thought I'd want to marry anyone, but that's changed. I want to be with you forever.*

I never thought I would get married, either. Why would I feel the need to have my love sanctioned by law? I had read (or partially read) Simone de Beauvoir's *The Second Sex* and

169

had fully adopted the idea that marriage was just a set of rules for things that should be spontaneous. Then there was all the abuse historically associated with marriage: women as property, women as housekeepers, women as sex slaves. Logically there's no reason for me to want to enter into a marriage contract. But I'm not behaving logically. I'm blinded by love and I'm ecstatic that Alex seems to feel the same way about me.

So we do get married. It's very low key. Alex thinks we should 'run away', go down to Gretna Green, do it quietly without telling anyone, without any fuss. I think this is a wonderfully romantic idea. Gretna Green is famous for its secret weddings. In the eighteenth century, an act was passed that meant couples under the age of twenty-one couldn't get married in England or Wales without their parents' permission. Those desperate enough would run away to Scotland, where the laws were different, and Gretna Green is right on the border. As it turns out, all the registrar offices in Gretna are fully booked for the rest of the year, so we go to Hawick instead, another border town. Afterwards, I phone my parents to tell them I just got married. *Married to who?* asks my mum.

For a while it doesn't change anything. We go to work during the day, we hang out in the house at night or go along to the Haymarket Bar or Diane's Pool Hall. It's only when I go down to London that it gets difficult. We're so far apart and neither of us has much money for travelling.

The first time Alex comes to London, it's a disaster. I'm staying in halls of residence and I'm not supposed to have visitors, even spousal ones, so Alex has to sneak in and out. We spend the nights squashed together in my single bed. Breakfast is provided with the halls of residence fees, so I go down to eat breakfast and to fill my pockets with anything I can take back to the room for Alex. Alex seems moody a lot of the time. He quizzes me about who I ate breakfast with, who I sat beside in lectures. I figure he's bored and lonely, spending so much time on his own, so I start to skip lectures to be with him.

One night, a few of the students I'm friendly with are going out to a pub in Camden. Alex and I go along too. He suggests we buy a half bottle of vodka so we don't have to pay the extortionate London prices for our drinks. We find a table in the pub and we all sit down together. Alex goes to the bar for a couple of Cokes and when he gets back he adds the vodka under the table. I'm a bit embarrassed, but nobody seems to notice what's going on.

I have what feels like a very precise memory of the horrors that occurred at the end of this evening, but I don't remember many earlier details: what the pub looked like, who said what, everyone who was there. What I do remember is a vague sense of apprehension.

It's something to do with the dislike Alex has for my student friends. He's met the people we're sitting with before and he's friendly enough towards them, but he's made it clear, privately, that he doesn't much like them. *Too loud and full of themselves*, he says. When we finish our drinks, I go up to the bar to get a couple more Cokes, vaguely anxious about leaving Alex at the table. He seems really pissed, even though we've just had one drink. While I'm waiting at the bar, Stuart, one of the other students, comes up to get drinks for himself and his friend Simon. We start chatting and he tells me a funny story about Simon's interaction with one of the tutors. I'm still smiling when I get back to the table.

What are you smiling about? says Alex. *What's so funny?*

Och, nothing really, I say, *just something Stuart said.*

Alex nods but says nothing. He adds the vodka to our glasses and sits in silence, drinking. Soon after, he says he wants to go and gets up. I follow him out to the carpark, saying a quick, embarrassed goodbye to my friends. As soon as we're outside, he turns on me. He's furious.

What the hell was that all about? he asks. *Oh Stuart, you're so funny . . . oh Stuart, I love you . . . oh Stuart, I wish I was married to YOU.*

I'm absolutely amazed. *Are you kidding?* I ask him. *We were chatting at the bar, he told me a funny story, that's all.*

You've spoken about him before, says Alex. *I knew you fancied him because of the way you talked about him. You've probably shagged him already.*

The whole scenario is so far-fetched I can hardly believe it. I'm angry, too. *For fuck's sake, Alex, he's a guy in a couple of my classes, I've spoken to him maybe ten times max. We get on okay but I barely know him. I do NOT fancy him, I have NOT shagged him, you're being completely ridiculous.*

Alex reaches out a hand and grabs me tight around the throat, right under my jaw, then he sort of runs me backwards until I hit the carpark wall. The knobbles of the pebble dash slam into my back.

Don't you ever call me ridiculous, you snooty cow, he snarls into my face. His other hand is raised in a fist as if he might punch me, but he doesn't. He lets go and takes a step back, breathing heavily.

I'm frightened now, and confused. I've never seen Alex like this; it's as if he's a different person. He turns and walks away. I stand there, shaking, staring at his back as it merges with the shadows on the other side of the carpark. After a few minutes he reappears, walking towards me. He looks worried.

Sorry, sorry, sorry, he's mumbling. *I'm drunk, don't know what got into me. It's just that it's really hard being so far away from you. I get scared about what might happen.*

I'm not immediately won over. *I can't do this, Alex,* I say. *I can't be with someone who hits me.*

But I didn't hit you, he says. *I would never hit you.*

Well, it looked to me like you might, I say. *And what you did was nasty enough. I was scared. I don't want to be with someone who scares me.*

I know, I know, I'm really sorry. He has tears in his eyes. *Please. You've got to believe me. This isn't me. I don't know what got into me. It won't happen again.*

Seriously, Alex, if it ever does, I'm gone, I reply. And I mean it. At the time, I mean it.

because I didn't believe that our toffee-apple romance could be rotten at the core, because I thought this anger was a one-off occurrence, that Alex was just in a strange place because of the strain of the long-distance relationship, because I was definitely not 'the type' to put up with being hit, because I would absolutely leave anyone who did that to me, because I believed in his repentance, his assurance that he would never hurt me, because to believe otherwise would have been devastating, because it would have meant that our exceptional, shining love was all scuffed-up and wrong, because I wasn't ready to accept that

CHAPTER 12

The Man sends me a Facebook message. Types of stalking behaviour

I didn't see The Man for two or three weeks, and congratulated myself on my special agent skills. I had basically turned into Jason Bourne, dodging around the city in a way that made me difficult to follow, senses highly attuned, looking at every stranger with suspicion, cutting through department stores and multi-storey carparks, using the lifts to change floors then going down the stairs and out a different exit. If I had had access to the city's sewers, I probably would have used them.

I also made sure I was never in the same place at the same time, with the exception of my son's school. I dropped him off there every morning and picked him up every afternoon. Apart from that, my movements were completely unpredictable. I never knew if The Man was somewhere nearby, watching me, waiting for an opportunity to approach when no one else was around, but it was a relief not to see him. I started to think maybe he had given up.

———

Then I got a Facebook message.

My insides turned to sludge as soon as I saw his name on the screen, my heart pumping quickfast horror into my veins. Like the email, the message was brief, and asked if we could meet up. I stared at the words, my fingers hovering over the keyboard, unsure what to do. My instinct was to delete them. I didn't want any scrap of this man anywhere in my life, and the message was like a mud-spattered flag on a battlefield, reminding me of his presence. But I didn't delete it.

Fortunately, I had an appointment with a counsellor later that day, and we used the CBT sheet to go through my reaction. The message had provoked fear, anger and a sense of powerlessness, triggered by the idea that there was no escape from this man, that no matter what I did, he would keep popping up in my life. This was supported by the fact that every time I thought he might have given up, there he was again, in the park, on my social media. But it was also true that I hadn't seen him in real life for several weeks. It could be that this was a last-ditch attempt to make contact, since I had made it so difficult for him to do that physically. This thought gave me hope that there was an end in sight.

We also spoke about what I should do next, how to regain a bit of control. When I had first gone to the police about The Man, they had told me to keep them updated with any developments, so I decided I would go back and tell them about the Facebook message.

———

Once again, the officer I spoke to was considerate and helpful.

There are a couple of things you could try, he said. *You could either reply and tell him to leave you alone, or you could just ignore him. There are pros and cons either way. If you tell him to leave you alone and he approaches you again, we can send someone to his house to caution him. Until you've told him you definitely don't want any contact, we can't do that. On the other hand, these people sometimes treat any kind of response as a win. Even if it's negative, any interaction might encourage them to keep going.*

Because I didn't know The Man, I had no idea how he would react. Was telling him to back off the right thing to do? He could just be someone who didn't pick up on subtle social cues, who needed me to be absolutely clear before he understood that I wasn't interested. Or he might be a complete sociopath who would be enraged by the rejection and come after me with a butcher's knife. Always keen to avoid conflict, especially ones that involved butcher's knives, I was inclined to ignore the message, but I knew this wasn't necessarily the right thing to do. It went against all the training I'd had from the patriarchy, but maybe I needed to be clearer about my own wants and needs. I decided to do a bit of research.

I found a few articles on what you should say to a persistent pursuer. They all suggested keeping it short and clear, not saying anything that could be misconstrued, not making it personal, and focusing on your own requirements. Keeping all this in mind, I wrote down my response. I kept it short, I didn't say anything personal, I focused on my own needs—but fear and uncertainty meant I couldn't quite build up the confidence to send it.

I had another look online for articles or papers that described different types of stalker to see if I could work out if responding was appropriate in my particular situation. The most useful document I came across was Spitzberg and Cupach's 'The state of the art of stalking',[1] which collates information from 175 different studies.

They explain one aspect of the stalking phenomenon by looking at the way that infants attach to their caregivers. If caregivers are indifferent or unresponsive, infants can become 'anxious ambivalent', i.e. they look for comfort from their caregivers, but whenever they get it, they become fearful that it will be withdrawn. This can lead to preoccupied attachment in later life. An 'anxious ambivalent' adult has a negative view of themselves, believing they're not worthy of comfort and support, and a positive view of others. They obsessively pursue the acceptance of others as a way of feeling better about themselves, but they also obsessively worry about eventual rejection from intimate partners. As a result, their relationships are often characterised by possessiveness and desperation and they have great difficulty handling relationship break-ups. Spitzberg and Cupach mention studies where large numbers of stalkers who had been imprisoned were found to have lost primary caregivers in their childhood. Many had also lost an important personal relationship in the six months prior to stalking.

Spitzberg and Cupach also identified eight different types of stalking behaviour, including hyper-intimacy (I thought of that first email with the personal details about lying in bed and the second encounter when The Man whispered

into my ear), mediated interactional contacts (communication via technology or appearing in different places
and making physical approaches), surveillance (attempting to secure information about the person without them
knowing, e.g. following and observing, or using computer
spyware) and harassment and intimidation (verbal or non-
verbal activities that deliberately annoy or stress the target).
More aggressive forms of stalking that I hadn't experienced
were invasion (e.g. breaking and entering, or stealing information), coercion and threat (explicit threat of harm) and
aggression (vandalism, use of a weapon, assault, attempted
or actual rape, attempted or actual homicide).

The paper also covered different ways that someone being
stalked might respond and how successful each was likely to
be. They divided the responses into five different categories:

1. Moving with—where the target tries to negotiate with the
   pursuer, politely requesting that they stop, or saying that
   they just want to be friends. This is hardly ever effective,
   as the pursuer is likely to convince themselves that there's
   still a chance of intimacy and redouble their efforts.
2. Moving against—where the target threatens the pursuer
   with the police or with violence from a third party. This
   is advised against because it increases the intensity of
   the situation as well as making the interaction public,
   which may infuriate the pursuer and 'elicit dangerous
   emotional reactions'.

3. Moving away—e.g. changing phone number, having mail sent to a PO box, blocking the pursuer on social media or shutting down accounts, always being with friends when in public and ignoring the pursuer when there is any attempt at interaction. This makes pursuit more difficult and time-consuming and experts generally agree that it's a necessary initial response.

4. Moving inward—where the target is in denial, pretending that there's no problem and attempting to relieve the stress by meditating, avoiding going out, self-medicating etc.

5. Moving outward—getting help from third parties (seeking counselling, reporting incidents to the police, moving in with a friend etc.)

Taking note that 'moving away' tactics seemed the most effective and that ignoring attempts at communication was advisable, I decided not to send the Facebook message I had prepared. It was a relief—I had been so anxious about it. Even though the message was basically just me being honest, my cultural training told me this sort of honesty was rude and confrontational.

I didn't know at the time that it would only be a matter of weeks before I needed to use the message in a more confrontational way than I had imagined. It was a situation that had my heart pumping wildly and my brain in chaos, so I was very glad I had a prepared statement that I had thought through.

Being married #1

I don't stay in London. It's too hard living so far from Alex. I convince myself that if we were together we would both be happier. He would be less moody, less jealous, less unsure of my love. After a year in London, I transfer to Edinburgh and change my degree to a Bachelor of Education.

We're ridiculously skint. To begin with we live in Alex's parents' house, but eventually we manage to get a council flat in Muirhouse. The area has a bad reputation—high crime, high unemployment, lots of drug use—but I like it. In between studying, I do a bit of work in Muirhouse Festival Arts Centre, helping to run drama classes and arts projects. When I'm there, I'm happy. I like the people, and work is a lot of fun.

When I go home, it's less fun. Alex has lost his job at the riding stables, and he's drinking a lot. I find empty vodka bottles stashed in drawers and coat pockets. When I ask him if he's started drinking through the day, he laughs. *I started drinking through the day when I was fourteen*, he says. *I'm just really good at hiding it.*

I can't believe I've been unaware of this the whole time we've been together. He tells me that when we lived in Haymarket he used to keep a half bottle hidden in the toilet cistern so he could nip off and have a drink whenever he wanted to. *Remember the big jar we used to keep all our change in?* he asks. *That kept me going in vodka when it got close to pay day.*

It's not all bad. Sometimes he's as warm and loving as he was when we first met. He still stops to kiss me when we pass each other in the hallway, we still lie together on the sofa, limbs entangled, we still have bright, shiny conversations. But I'm learning to censor what I say. If I mention a previous relationship, or any male friend, the conversation can flip. To begin with it's just a change of mood, a dark silence, but soon he's subtly undermining me.

You know, I could get jealous of your friend Malcolm, but I realise it's highly unlikely he would fancy you.

Those jeans look a bit tight, have you put on weight again?

It's weird how Shona hates you so much. I keep telling her you're lovely, really, but she still goes on about how annoying you are.

Gradually the undermining becomes less subtle. One night, when he's been drinking, he asks me, quite casually, how many other people I've slept with. I try to remember how many I've told him about. I think it's three, so I tell him three. *My god, so that's four including me*, he says. *And you're only twenty-three. What a complete slut. And then there's all the others you're not telling me about. You're such a whore. I can't believe I married such a whore.*

My anxiety ramps up. Most of the time I'm treading on eggshells, trying not to break any but finding it impossible. I always seem to do or say something wrong. And if Alex can't find anything immediate to complain about, he brings up my past.

Sex becomes nerve-racking. He's still loving and gentle to begin with, but often he'll stop halfway through, suddenly furious. *I can't get that picture of you and . . . out of my head! Why did you have to be such a whore! It's spoilt everything!*

When he's had a lot to drink, it's far worse. A pattern emerges. He gets smashed, screams insults at me, punches walls, physically restrains me in various ways. The next day he's aghast at what he's done and profusely apologetic. *Please don't leave me, I couldn't live without you. I can't expect you to forgive me when I can't forgive myself, but please don't turn your back on me.*

I inevitably say I'll give him one last chance and things are easier for a while, at least until he gets his next dole cheque. He goes off to the post office to cash it in and I don't see him for the rest of the day. When he comes back, he's so legless he can barely stand upright. He sways on his feet, gouching at me, his mouth hanging open. His speech is almost incomprehensible. Before long his eyes get hard and cold, and I know what's coming.

I start to live in fear of the fortnightly payments. I try to guess when he'll come back and I leave the house, waiting until I think he's had enough time to get back and fall asleep. Often I get it wrong, go home too early and find he's still awake. Of course he wants to know where I've been and who I've been speaking to, and whatever the answer is, he's angry. And so the cycle continues.

The violence gradually creeps in. He knows how much my extensive vinyl collection means to me, so one day when

I'm out at work, he methodically goes through the whole lot, taking each record out of its sleeve and smashing it with a hammer.

I tell him I'm sick of him undermining me, and he slaps me hard across the face.

To get away from him during an argument, I lock myself in the bathroom, and he kicks the door in and drags me out by my hair.

Still I don't leave.

One night, we've come back from the pub and we're listening to music in the sitting room. It's during the easy period between dole cheques and things are going well. We've had two pints in the pub and we've brought a couple of cans home with us. Alex is on the sofa, feet stretched out in front of him, arms spread across the back of it. He still has his jacket and shoes on. He's telling me some story about the band and although I've heard it before, I'm laughing along. I'm lying on the floor, propped up on one elbow, my jacket and shoes in a heap beside me. We talk about the old days, when we lived in Haymarket, when our lives were full of music. For no apparent reason, Alex starts to question me about what I did when I was in London and he wasn't there. Within minutes he's raging. Nothing can persuade him that I wasn't sleeping my way around the university. I try to stay calm and this seems to enrage him even more. Suddenly he jumps up from the sofa, strides towards me, swings his leg back and kicks me in the face.

There's blackness, haziness, a lot of noise, a lot of struggle. I manage to grab my jacket and shoes as I scramble to my feet. I somehow manage to get out of the house. I run, I think, for a long time. I end up at my brother's house. I tell him what has happened and he goes back to my house and rings the bell, and when Alex answers the door he punches him in the face. I stay behind, curled up in a ball in the corner of my brother's sitting room as my eye slowly swells into a purple and green golf ball with a closed slit across the middle. At this point, I don't know how bad it looks. I don't have a mirror.

because it was such a gradual thing, because I kept putting up with a little bit more and a little bit more, because I was basically groomed to accept it, because there were still good times when everything seemed okay, when I thought we were still in love, because my self-esteem was being slowly eroded and I'd started to believe I was worthless, because I couldn't tell anyone what was happening, because I was ashamed of being that person, a woman who stayed with a man who hit her, because I believed he really was sorry, because I believed he wanted to change, because I thought if I just did everything right, if I kept quiet about things that annoyed him and helped him to cut down on drinking, then things would get better, because bad things had been done to him as a child, because he had learnt his behaviour from his father, because I don't think the grooming or manipulation was conscious, because I think he'd been taught that that was just what men did, because I knew he hated himself far more than I hated him

CHAPTER 13

Confronting The Man. He turns up at my son's school

I had planned to meet a friend for coffee after dropping my son off at school. It was a few weeks after the Facebook message and I hadn't heard anything more from The Man. Despite my past experiences, I had once again convinced myself that he must be fed up with my lack of response and that the months of anxiety were now over.

When my son and I cycled to school I had been avoiding our usual route, which went along the street that I had walked down with The Man after the park incident. I couldn't look at those houses, the pink rosebushes, without the ghost of him haunting my thoughts, rattling the stones inside me. But this particular morning I had unthinkingly taken the old route and we were cycling along, playing Twenty Questions and enjoying the early morning sunshine on our backs. It was only when we were standing at the school gates that I realised I had gone the whole way without once thinking about The Man. It felt like an important achievement.

I waved goodbye as my son ran off into the playground, schoolbag bouncing on his back. I couldn't remember where I was supposed to meet my friend, so I hung around the gates for a bit, hoping to catch her as she dropped off her son. There were one or two other parents around, but it was nearly time for school to start, so most had come and gone. My friend was probably in the café by now, waiting for me to turn up.

The sun was getting hotter so I moved into the crochet of shade under a jacaranda tree. A warm breeze blew clumps of its lavender blossoms around my feet as I got out my phone. *This is Bumbleheid,* I texted my friend, *which café again?*

Just as I was searching for the question mark, I heard someone call my name. I looked up and saw a man on a bike, waving. There were roadworks just outside the school and he had pulled up on the other side of them. I figured it must be the dad of one of the kids in my son's class, but I couldn't tell which one. The sun was behind him and he was too far away. I shouted hello and waved back, then carried on with the text. Just as I was about to hit send, some synapse in my brain clicked into place.

Shit, that wasn't one of the dads, it was him! It was The Man!

Instantly my mood changed. All the carefree freedom of the cycle to school, all the joy of chatting with my son and looking forward to meeting my friend were gone. The stones rattled wildly as the familiar sense of panic set in. I was going to have to resign myself to this for the rest of my life, this ongoing pursuit by a person I didn't know, the fear of what he might do next, it was never going to end, there was nothing I could do to make it stop.

He was still there, waiting in the road like a malevolent spirit in a bike helmet. What was he waiting FOR? Did he think I WANTED to speak to him? Or didn't what I want concern him, didn't he think it was worthy of consideration?

At this point, something inside me snapped. I was so sick of it all. Sick of tiptoeing around the male ego, sick of being polite for fear of offending anyone, sick of subjugating my own needs in order to fulfil someone else's expectations. I was going to let The Man know how I felt, whatever the consequences.

My insides were like jelly, but I tried to keep the outside calm. I drew myself up and walked purposefully in his direction. *This is it,* I was thinking, *enough is enough. It's time to do the speech.* In my head, I went over the Facebook message I had prepared. Four sentences. Surely it couldn't be that hard to say four sentences.

He was still sitting on the bike, relaxed and grinning, one foot on the ground, the other on a pedal. I kept my face serious as I got closer, and I started speaking as soon as I reached him. I didn't want him to distract me with pseudo-friendly chatter.

I'm going to say this really clearly so there can't be any misunderstanding, I said. *I don't want to speak to you. I don't want you to contact me in any way. I just want you to leave me alone.*

The grin slid from his face. *Oh!* he said, as if completely taken aback. *Oh, okay.* He didn't argue, he didn't spit at me, he didn't threaten or verbally abuse me. He just turned away and cycled off.

I stood for a minute, watching him grow smaller in the road.

Was that it? Was it really that simple? He had seemed genuinely surprised. Maybe he really had thought I was interested in him, that his advances were welcomed. Maybe all that had been required, all this time, was for me to be clear about my position. I wondered if I had misjudged everything, made a mountain out of a molehill.

Then my phone pinged. Sunlight bounced off the screen, filling my eyes with its brightness. I cupped my hand around it and peered in. It was my friend.

Cibo, doofus, the text said.

I smiled. When I looked up from the screen, The Man was just a dot at the end of the street. I turned in the opposite direction and started walking towards the café, and for the first time in a long time, I felt strong.

Being married #2

The day after Alex gives me a black eye, my brother suggests I stay with him for a while. I agree that it's a good idea, but I'm supposed to be starting a new job the following day. I have a temporary position in the bar at the Highland Show. I feel lucky to have got the job—lots of people applied. Even though I've had several years' experience of bartending, it feels like they must have made a mistake. That's how low my self-esteem is at this stage. I can't believe anyone would pick me.

It's only for a few days, and the bar will be insanely busy, but the money is really good. I can't afford not to show up. This means I'm going to have to go back to the house to get my work clothes. My brother asks if I want him to go instead, but I say no. I'm not worried about Alex, I know the pattern. I'm not in any danger. Not physically, at least.

Right enough, when I go back to the house, Alex is shocked at what he's done to my eye and desperately apologetic. He's been crying all night, he says. He doesn't know what happened, he's never done anything like that before and he won't ever do it again. He's glad my brother punched him in the face, he knows he deserved it. He's going to get help with his drinking. He's spoken to a doctor and there's a program he can go on. He has to take tablets called Antabuse that will make him really sick if he touches alcohol, but he needs someone to help him, to make sure that he takes them every day. He really needs me, please, please, please can't

I help him with this? There's no one else he can turn to and he really wants to get better.

I tell him I'll think about it.

The next day, I go to work at the Highland Show with a neat white blouse and a neat black skirt and a huge swollen eye. I feel overwhelmed with shame. I know this is not a good look for someone serving G&Ts to the well-to-do. I've tried to cover up the bruising with make-up, but there's no hiding the swelling, the slit eye. The other bar staff chat and laugh and flirt with each other, while I keep my head down and try not to make eye contact. I cringe every time someone asks what happened to my eye, but I feel worse when people don't ask. I don't want them thinking I'm a 'battered wife'.

———

Years later, while writing this book, I hear American author Dr Jackson Katz[1] talking about how the use of passive language, particularly around men's violence against women, has the effect of absolving men of blame. He mentions a linguistic exercise he has developed to illustrate this. It starts with the sentence 'John beat Mary', which changes to become 'Mary was beaten by John'. The focus has already shifted from John to Mary, because Mary is now the subject of the sentence. It changes again to 'Mary was beaten', then 'Mary was battered', then 'Mary is a battered woman'. The sequence illustrates how the use of passive language changes what John did to Mary into something that is now Mary's identity, something that she seems responsible for because John is no longer part of the conversation, it's just who Mary is.

Of course, I don't know any of this at the time. All I know is that being a 'battered wife' is a shameful thing. I don't want to be that thing and I've therefore convinced myself that it's not what's happening, that with Alex and I, it's different. Avoiding the clichéd 'walked-into-a-door', 'fell-down-the-stairs' excuses, I tell everyone I got mugged by a couple of guys who ran off with my bag. I don't think anyone believes me.

Later, when I'm waiting in a queue to buy myself some lunch, the bar manager is standing behind me. He points to the purse in my hand.

Lucky that wasn't in your bag when it was stolen, he says.

I mumble something about having more than one purse, but the heat in my face must be a giveaway.

I spend the rest of my lunchbreak in the toilets, crying. I feel stupid and lonely and different. I don't belong in this bar with these bouncy, happy, flirty people and their unblemished faces, their unblemished lives. I just want to go home, but I don't know where home is.

———

Of course, I move back in with Alex. Of course, for a while, everything is fine. Alex starts taking Antabuse and he seems to be coping really well. He gets a job as a stagehand in a theatre. It seems like he's really making an effort, and I begin to think things might work out. But after a couple of months, Alex decides he doesn't need the Antabuse anymore. He's got things under control, he says, he can have a little drink now and again without it getting out of hand.

Inevitably, it does get out of hand. Not during the day, not when he's working, but if we go for a night out, he gets absolutely hammered. I hate it, especially if we're out with friends. It's embarrassing being with someone who's so drunk nobody can understand what they're saying, who's so drunk they bang into several people on their way to the bar and don't even notice, who's so drunk they get nasty and abusive for no reason.

I start going out without him. If I've been working at the arts centre and people are going to the pub afterwards, I go with them without phoning him or going home first. I feel more relaxed, more able to be myself, when he's not there. Something opens up inside me. I feel a little less invisible, a little less pathetic.

One evening, I'm at home getting ready for a night out. Alex has gone for a drink with his workmates, so I'm taking my time, showering, putting on make-up. I'm sitting on the side of the bed drying my hair when I hear his key in the door. I can tell, by the amount of time it takes him to get in, that he's plastered. There's a clatter as he stumbles over the hoover that's been left out in the hallway, then he's there in the bedroom doorway, swaying on his feet, grinning.

Hey, he says, *you're going out. Where are you off to?*

I'm just going to meet some folk from work, I say, raising my voice above the rush of the hairdryer.

Right, he says. *Where are you meeting them?*

The Gunner, I say. It's a lie, but I don't want him turning up at The Doo'cot, which is where I'm really going.

Great, he says. *I'll come with you.*

I clench my jaw. *I don't think that's a good idea*, I say. *We'll just be talking about work, it'll be really boring. And anyway, you're pissed already.*

I'm not THAT drunk, he says. *It'll be fine.*

I finish off drying my hair. I don't say anything. I'm wondering how I'm going to get out of the house without Alex following me. In the end I decide I just have to be straight with him. I unplug the dryer. *To be honest, Alex, I just don't want you to come*, I say as I wind up the cord. *You're pissed already, you're just going to get more pissed, and I'll end up having to look after you. It's no fun for me when we're out and you're plastered.*

Come off it, Alex says. *You're going to the pub. Everyone'll be pissed.*

Aye, but nobody'll be as pissed as you. I walk towards the bedroom door, but he puts his hand on the doorframe, barring the way. His eyes have gone flat, cold.

If I'm not going, you're not going, he says.

I must be feeling reckless, because I actually laugh and push past him. I put the hairdryer away in the sitting-room cupboard and I pick up my bag from the sofa. He's right behind me.

I mean it, you selfish cow, you're not going anywhere. I know you think you can sneak off without me, you're probably planning on shagging someone, but I'm not going to let you. You're not getting out of this house.

I'm nervous now, but I'm not backing down. My fingernails grip into the material of my bag. My coat and shoes are by the front door, if I can just grab them on my way out . . . I move towards the hall but he jumps in front of me, smirking. I try to get past but he shoves hard, both hands on my shoulders, pushing me back. I run at him, wild, furious, but this time he's more forceful, throwing me to the floor. He's the one who's laughing now. He crouches down, his face close to mine. *You're such a stupid cow,* he says. *Do you really think you can get out if I don't want you to? You're far too weak.*

In a frenzy, I leap up, sending him off balance so that he sits down hard on the floor. His hands grab at me as I step over him, but I break free and make a run for the hall. He scrambles onto all fours and launches himself towards me in a sort of rugby tackle, grabbing my ankles. My bag flies out of my hands and lipstick, keys, wallet somersault through the air. I crash to the floor. There's a crack as my forehead smacks off the abandoned hoover.

I lie there for a minute, dazed, my head throbbing, then I roll over onto my back. Alex crawls towards me, is on his hands and knees above me. He's in tears.

No,no,no,no,no,no,no, he's saying. *Look what you've made me do to you. Why couldn't you just let me come to the pub?*

I wasn't asking for much, just to go out with you. He strokes my hair. *You're bleeding,* he says. *I'm sorry, I'm so sorry, I didn't mean to do this, you can see it was just an accident. The problem is I love you too much.*

I raise myself up on my elbows. I look into the blue, blue of his teary eyes. *Can you get off me, please,* I say. *I want to stand up.*

He moves aside, watching as I roll over onto all fours. I wait for the pain in my head to subside before getting slowly to my feet and going into the bathroom. I lean on the basin and stare at myself in the mirror. There's a dark hole in my forehead. Blood is running down my face, collecting in my eyebrow, my eyelashes, trickling on down my cheek. I get some wet tissue and I try to clean it up, but more blood keeps coming. Eventually I realise it's not going to stop, not with a bit of wet tissue. I fold loo roll into a pad and hold it against the hole. I go out into the hallway. Alex is sitting on the floor with his back against the wall and his head in his hands.

It won't stop bleeding, I say. *I think it needs stitches. I'm going to have to go to the hospital.*

Alex lifts his head, looks up at me. He starts to get to his feet. *I'll come with you,* he says.

No, I say. *I don't want you to.*

He slumps back down. *Okay,* he says, *okay.*

I pick up all the things that are scattered down the hallway and put them back in my bag. I put on my coat and shoes, and open the front door.

———

It's when I'm sitting in a cubicle in the hospital, waiting to be stitched up, that I realise it's over. Again, I've had to lie about what's happened. *Tripped over the cat and landed on the hoover.* Four stitches. I can no longer deny that I am that woman. It occurs to me that if I don't leave Alex, he might end up killing me.

Afterwards, I get the bus back to Muirhouse, but I get off at the Doo'cot, hoping that some of the folk from work might still be there. A few of them are, including Jackie, a woman I know only slightly. She's about ten years older than me and lives on her own with her daughter. She's the sort of person people would describe as 'salt of the earth'. Big heart, big laugh. If I'm honest, I'm slightly intimidated by her.

She looks up as I come in.

Holy shit, she says. *What the fuck happened to you?*

I sit down beside her. I tell her what happened. I tell her I feel sick when I think about going back to the house, but I don't know where else to go. I'm too ashamed to let my parents or my friends know what's been going on. I don't want my brother to get into a fight with Alex.

Right, hen, she says, flinging an arm around me. *Fuck that shit. You're coming home with me.*

Tough and sweary as she is, it's as if Jackie has been sent from heaven. Basically, she saves me. For a few months, until I sort out somewhere permanent to stay, she's my guardian angel. I move into her spare room. Instead of charging me rent, she gets me to babysit her daughter once a week so that she can go for a girls' night out. We take it in turns to cook, clean, shop, do the laundry. Most nights, we sit in front of the telly, smoking and drinking and laughing our heads off. She tells me about her own violent relationship with her daughter's father, a man she still sees on account of joint custody.

We're alright now, she says. *Now that I don't have to live with the fucker.*

In the past, I would have been amazed that someone as resilient and strong as Jackie would ever put up with a man hitting her. But I know now that it's not that simple.

because you don't have to be weak or crazy to end up with a violent partner, because it's not that unusual, because 'worldwide, almost one third of women who have been in a relationship report that they have experienced . . . physical and/or sexual violence by (an) intimate partner',[2] because stereotypes mean we tend to think that all women who are beaten by their partners are passive/naïve/poorly educated/ in denial, because the violence is not the only thing a woman might have to worry about, because homelessness, poverty, lack of stability in her children's lives or being stigmatised might also need to be considered, because it's not the same for every woman, because cultural, social and economic differences mean each situation has to be considered separately,[3] because not everyone has the necessary support networks to allow them to leave, because many women who live with violent men actually show great strength and resilience in their ability to manage their situation

CHAPTER 14

The Man appears in my local café. Misogyny and young women

Needless to say, it wasn't the end of The Man's appearances. A week or so later, I had done the usual school drop-off and was heading towards one of my favourite cafés. As I got closer, I saw The Man sitting at a table, just outside the door. I made a quick detour, glancing in his direction as I walked past. He was watching me. He didn't smile. He didn't say hello.

What did this mean? Was he angry with me for what I'd said? If he'd got the message that I didn't want to speak to him, why was he still hanging round? I could feel the fear clawing its way from my stomach up to my throat.

As luck would have it, there was a police station quite near the café. It wasn't the same station I'd been to before, so I had to explain the situation to the officer. I told her what I'd said to The Man outside the school, that he'd seemed surprised and had just cycled away. *But now he's sitting outside a café that I quite often go to*, I continued. *He lives on the other side of town, so I don't see why he would be here.*

He might just be making a point, the officer said. *If stalking is his modus operandi, he probably knows what the rules are. There actually isn't anything we can do about him sitting in a café. Now that you've told him you don't want any contact, if he tries to speak to you, or sends you any more messages, we can get a couple of officers to go round to his house. One of them will caution him and the other one will video it. That's usually enough to put people*

*off. They don't like being videoed. But he's not breaking
the law by being in this area if he isn't trying to speak to
you. Unfortunately, that's just something you have to put
up with.*

Having once again believed that it was all over, this was
a bit of a blow. I had thought that by explaining my position
I had cleared up a misunderstanding. The Man finally knew
what I wanted, what I needed, and now we would both
move on. But it seemed The Man wasn't ready to move on.
How long was he prepared to hang around here? What else
was he prepared to do? Had I made him so angry he might
try and punish me in some way?

I had swung so quickly from thinking I might be making
mountains out of molehills to thinking there was a possibility my life was in danger. I had always considered myself
an optimist, a glass half-full sort of person. Why were there
suddenly so many rattling stones inside me? Maybe the
stones weren't just rattling for The Man. Maybe they were
rattling for all the men, for all the incidents in my life when a
man had treated me badly or taken advantage because I was
a woman. Maybe they were rattling because of all the other
women I had heard or read about, women who had been
stalked, beaten, killed by men who thought, at the time,
that it was their right to do these things. As I sat there telling
my story to the police officer, I was suddenly hit by the tidal
wave of incidents—the objectification, the undermining,
the overruling, the underplaying, the background noise of

misogyny I had been hearing all my life. It had carried me here, to this police station, hoping that the forces of law and order would help me find a way to put an end to the intrusion. Instead I was now realising that there was nothing to be done. I was living in a world still governed by patriarchal rules, still insisting that women (and men, people of any gender) behave in particular ways, still punishing them if they didn't. I felt utterly powerless and amazed at how much I'd been ignoring, how hardened I had become to the microaggressions.

I guess it's the same for all of us. We live with sexism and misogyny and we get used to it. We shouldn't have to, but we do. Over the course of our lives, we build up a mental resilience, a kind of denial, but it takes it toll.

Awareness begins to creep in during adolescence. The Longitudinal Study of Australian Children's *Annual Statistical Report 2016*[1] found that girls were almost four times more likely to self-harm than boys. Although the report attributed this to 'issues related to pubertal development', journalist Ellie Mae O'Hagan points out in an article in *The Guardian*[2] that the huge gender divide needs to be addressed more fully. 'Women, in general, are taught to hurt themselves in a multitude of ways: by hating their bodies, by having low expectations of relationships, by subjugating their own needs to those of others, and by viewing male approval as a form of validation,' she says. 'Little wonder, then, that the response of many women is to turn pain inwards.'

In addition, women are encouraged to believe that any unhappiness they experience is due to their own failings. And because we're also taught that male acceptance is an important life goal, it's very difficult for us to complain to men about their behaviour.

What's more, the teenage girl, as seen in the media, is stereotyped as someone who constantly frets over her appearance and seeks approval from boys. She's often shown as a shallow 'princess' or 'bimbo', despite the fact that this is exactly the behaviour the patriarchy demands from her. Damned if she does, damned if she doesn't. It's a lot for a young girl to take onboard. As O'Hagan says, 'until we can be honest about the fact that misogyny plays a crucial role in the lives of teenage girls, they will continue to suffer in ways that their male counterparts simply do not'. And of course, this is just the start of it. The objectification, the undermining, the gender expectations don't stop after adolescence. They carry on, and they have an impact on our mental, and often physical, health.

I asked Action Against Stalking's Ann Moulds about the long-term effects of stalking in particular. She told me:

There's no specific research out there, but obviously there's a psychological, emotional, financial and social impact.

Psychologically it changes a person's worldview, that erosion of trust. 'I thought I was safe', 'I believed

I was in control of my life', those are the sort of belief systems that many of us live with. Stalking can catapult a person into another reality that they can't make sense of, and they don't have the coping strategies to manage it. It forces a person to look at their own vulnerabilities and that changes a person forever. And these massive existential changes that stalking forces on a person forever are going unrecognised. The impact of that.

When the stalking goes on for any length of time, living with that fear, living with uncertainty around what's going to happen next, living with loss of control and erosion of safety, there's a much higher level of anxiety and then you get the cortisol effect, which can destroy the nervous system and exacerbate existing conditions or trigger new conditions. There are certainly links to the cortisol effect and cancer. It's so important to try and help victims manage anxiety so they're not as at risk from these long-term effects.

I know exactly what Anne's talking about. Shortly after being stalked, I noticed a sudden increase in joint pain. It was painful to hold a book up to read when I was lying in bed, to carry bags of shopping back from the supermarket. When it started to affect my ability to do the cleaning and polishing necessary for my work upcycling furniture, I went to the doctor. I was diagnosed with rheumatoid arthritis and, some months later, osteoporosis, which often goes hand in hand with joint inflammation. As far as I know, no one in my extended family suffers, or has suffered, from either of these normally hereditary conditions. As I came to the end of writing this book, I received a further, devastating diagnosis: stage 4 cancer, a rare and aggressive kind that is likely to kill me in the next couple of years. I have no hard evidence that this is a direct result of being stalked, or raped, or living with domestic violence, but I do know that none of this could have helped.

Caroline Madden is a bodyworker and Bowen Technique practitioner who has studied human anatomy and chronic conditions for more than fifteen years. I spoke to her about the connection between stress and physical health.

'There's a lot of interest in the vagus nerve at the moment,' she told me, 'lots of scientific papers coming out on the most recent findings.' She explained that the vagus nerve is the epicentre of mind-body interaction. It forms a pathway between the brain and the digestive tract, sending messages from gut to brain in times of stress or anxiety (hence the term 'gut instinct'). It's the main component of the parasympathetic nervous system, regulating activity in the heart and lungs as well as the digestive system, and controlling immune function and inflammatory responses. When a person is in a state of hyper-arousal, activity in the vagus nerve causes a decrease in heart rate, blood pressure, muscle tone, depth of breath, social engagement and, importantly, immune response. On the plus side, healthy vagal tone will reduce hyper-arousal, helping you realise when danger has passed and keeping you calm when you're under stress. Not surprisingly, the optimum functioning of this nerve is key to both physical and mental health and therefore longevity.

A vagus nerve stimulator, implanted in the chest, is one way of keeping the nerve healthy and active, and the device has recently been approved for the treatment of chronic depression. However, there are less invasive ways of stimulating the nerve. Caroline gave me a couple of exercises I could do at home.

'A good breathing exercise for the vagus nerve is to breathe in for four seconds, hold for four seconds, breathe out for four, hold for four. Let your inbreath fill your lungs, expanding the stomach, and let your outbreath empty your lungs completely. Try to do this through your nose, with your mouth closed, as nitric oxide is released with nose breathing and that's good for your blood vessels. It's a signal to the vessels to relax and expand which gets blood, oxygen and nutrients flowing to every part of your body.

'You can also exercise the suboccipital nerves at the back of your skull which are associated with stress and headaches. Either lying on your back or sitting up, clasp your hands behind your head, near the base of the skull, or just rest your fingers on the back of your head with the thumbs pressing lightly on the base of the skull. Keeping your head straight, look as far right as is comfortable and hold it for half a minute to a minute. Then do the same thing, looking to the left.'

Probiotics and Omega-3 are good for vagal tone too, as is meditation, singing or humming and plunging your face into cold water to stimulate the diving response.

In *The Body Keeps the Score*,[3] Bessel van der Kolk also talks about how the body is changed physically and mentally when exposed to trauma and stress, particularly if we have no outlet for our emotions. Without good vagal tone, these changes can remain in the body and leave us vulnerable to all kinds of auto-immune diseases, including cancer. This has particular significance for women, who are at greater risk of experiencing sexual abuse and/or domestic violence in their lifetimes, but the implications are much wider. Children who live with domestic violence or neglect frequently have no way of processing the resulting trauma and therefore end up living with high levels of stress and often a disturbed view of themselves or the world. Van der Kolk argues that if things are to change, we need to go to the root of the problem and help parents with their mental health issues, addictions, poverty or isolation. The result would be fewer children growing up with stress and the associated health conditions as well as the type of mental health issues that can lead to abusive patterns of behaviour. Financially, an investment in parenting programs for disad-vantaged families could save the US billions every year in health and criminal justice costs. Addressing the sexism and misogyny at the centre of patriarchal cultures would presumably have a similar effect.

While shopping

I'm shopping with my daughter, who needs an outfit for a party. We wander into a jeans shop that's pumping out rap music. Heavy bass. 'Phat beats,' we would have said, back in the day. I like the rhythm of it and find myself nodding in time as I watch my daughter riffling through racks of clothes. I catch one of the lines of the song and stop nodding, start listening. The rapper is explaining how he dealt with one of his 'bitches' when he caught her stealing money from him. According to the lyrics, he smashed her face against a mirror and threw her to the floor, causing her skirt to ride up so he could see her knickers. This got him excited. He hit her again and then he got his dick out and rammed it repeatedly into her mouth, trying to choke her. I feel choked myself, listening to this. My throat is thick with anger. I can't believe it's being played in a public space. I don't want to draw my daughter's attention to it, but on the other hand, she's not deaf. I don't want to let it pass unremarked either.

Have you heard what's coming out of the speakers? I ask her.

She rolls her eyes. *I know, right?* she says.

I look around. I'm the oldest person in the shop by at least twenty years. Young women, some still girls, are milling about, picking up shirts and skirts, looking at them, showing them to each other, laughing, checking their phones. They seem oblivious to the misogynistic hate-speech going on around them. I hope it's oblivion and not just acceptance, a shoulder-shrugging 'That's just the way it is.' The disempowered youth. I feel strangely protective of them, outraged that they should have to listen to this. It's the outrage of a middle-aged woman who has spent many years voicing discontent (though not voicing enough), who thought, by now, things might have changed. What does this do to you if you're a young woman on the cusp of adulthood, just trying on your woman shoes? Subconsciously, what does it do? What does it do to young men? I imagine my son listening to this vocalisation of toxic machismo. I know he would find it upsetting and I would want to protect him too, protect all the young people who might be impacted by this. I want to go to the counter and ask if they realise what they're playing. I say this to my daughter.

Oh god, Mum, PLEASE don't, she says.

So I don't. Maybe I wouldn't have anyway. Years of conditioning.

because misogyny and the gender divide makes life difficult for girls AND boys, but especially girls, because around puberty, girls are almost twice as likely as boys to suffer from depression (32 per cent of girls compared to 18 per cent of boys), because girls are more than twice as likely to suffer from anxiety (34 per cent of girls compared to 13 per cent of boys),[4] because puberty brings about a much greater awareness of the way women are viewed in society, because teenage girls are bombarded with sexualised imagery and commentary that encourages them to look at their own bodies with distaste, because, unlike boys, they learn that their own needs and desires must come second to the needs and desires of others if they want to win approval, because, unlike boys, they learn that being liked, being a nice person, is more important than being respected, because, unlike boys, they are shamed when they complain so they learn to internalise their anger, because, unlike boys, they learn to take responsibility for other people's happiness

CHAPTER 15

An overseas reprieve.
The difficulty of
prosecuting stalkers

As it turned out, I didn't have to worry about The Man for too much longer. The stones could settle back into the gravelly pit at the bottom of my stomach.

This was partly to do with my own circumstances. I was suffocating in the mud of homesickness. Stuck on the other side of the world, I had missed my parents' golden wedding anniversary and the birth of my niece (my brother's first child, whom I still hadn't met). Not being there for these big family events had clogged my insides with a coagulated mass of emotion. We had also realised we couldn't afford to hang on to our home in Scotland, the terraced house that looked out across an island-strewn bay where teaspoons of light spilt through the clouds and splashed down among the waves. It was hard to let go. Letting go meant saying goodbye to that brick-and-mortar album of memories, goodbye to the idea that one day we might go back, take up our old lives, once again be the people we were when we lived there.

I was being absurdly nostalgic, of course. And these were such privileged problems, considering the millions who have nothing of their old lives left, no chance of returning, even for a visit, who have only a temporary refugee camp to call home, or cardboard and a sleeping bag in a doorway. It helped to remind myself of this, of how lucky I really was, but my insides still twisted like a tourniquet when I thought of my parents, my sister, my brother, the life I had left behind.

We didn't have enough money for a family trip, but we decided that I should go back on my own for a month, to clear out the homesickness inside me and to clear out the possessions we had left in the house. My partner would take our son to school, the bairns could help out with cleaning and meals.

I went back for the month of November. When I returned to Australia, there were only a couple of weeks of school left before the Christmas holidays. I didn't see The Man during that time or during the six weeks of holiday. Since I had most frequently seen him just after school drop-off, I figured he had either decided to back off when I made my feelings clear to him, or he'd gotten fed up trying to find me during my absence. I did see him once, months and months later, cycling down Prospect Road. This time there was no blood-thump of horror, no rattle of stones. *Oh, there's that man again*, was the tiny thought that slipped through my brain, almost unnoticed.

I was lucky. It could have been so much worse.

In 2018 the UK women's network Broadly launched their Unfollow Me campaign to raise awareness of stalking. They found that from 2015 to 2017 forty-nine women in the UK had been murdered by men they had previously reported to the police. The Broadly website shares the stories of some of the women. It makes for difficult reading.[1] The campaign also highlights the fact that in the UK, there is currently no way of monitoring serial stalkers or perpetrators of domestic violence. The same is true of Australia, as I found out when I first went to the police. What's worse here is that someone convicted of these crimes only needs to move interstate if he wants his (or her) criminal record to become difficult to access. By the Legal Services Commission of South Australia's own admission, 'it is very difficult to prove a person is guilty of stalking as the police will have to show . . . that the "stalker" *intended* to cause either:

- serious mental or physical harm to another person or a third person, or
- serious apprehension or fear'.[2]

Not surprisingly, the number of stalking cases dismissed far outweighs the number of convictions. Something clearly needs to be done if the one in five women who experience stalking at some point in their lives[3] are to feel a little safer.

Earlier stalking research, supported by the Criminology Research Council (Australia), found there was a need to address weaknesses in the legal system, train police officers, focus on long-term intervention strategies and find out more about community awareness.[4] Some of these strategies have since been put in place. The training of police officers in SAPOL (South Australian Police), for example, made a huge difference to my experience of reporting the stalking. However, the report also pointed out that males usually view stalking less seriously than do females, a situation that hasn't changed much. This has huge implications for the decisions being made by male jurors and magistrates in court.

ELLIS GUNN

The report concluded that it was most important 'for stalking to be recognised by police, magistrates and the general public as a crime which impinges upon the lives of ordinary people in ways which are threatening, invasive and potentially dangerous'.

Having a drink with friends

I'm having a drink with some women friends in Adelaide. There are seven of us sitting at a long wooden table outside a pub in Hindley Street. We've just been to a conference on intersectionality and we're talking about what we've heard, what we've learnt. As the wine flows, the conversation moves on to sexual harassment.

Whatever happened to flashers? someone says. Remember the days when you got flashed at every other week?

Maybe not as much as every other week, but as we chat, we realise we've all had multiple experiences, mostly as children and adolescents, of men exposing their genitals to us. We're all well over thirty, so we don't know if the recent decrease in incidents is because it doesn't happen so much these days, or if it's because men who like to expose themselves generally target younger women and girls. We all remember the trauma, the feeling of disgust, of having been violated without being touched. None of us told anyone what had happened. We felt too ashamed. We didn't want anyone to know what our eyes had seen. We didn't want the filth of it in our mouths.

We also remember that flashers were seen by the media as a bit of a joke. They often appeared in comedy sketches, the 'dirty old man in a raincoat'. They were laughed at rather than reviled. Even the word—'flasher'—belies the distress imposed on the target, trivialises the offence and the trauma.

Someone tells a story about a share house she once lived in. There was a guy in a house directly opposite who would regularly expose himself at his window. She would be taking out the bins, thoughtfully staring up at the sky, wondering what she was going to have for lunch maybe, and then she'd catch sight of him at his upstairs window, looking down at her while he masturbated. Ugh. It really made her skin crawl, she said. She would see him in the street sometimes and he would scurry past, not catching her eye. She thought he was probably embarrassed, but a few days later, there he'd be again, at his window, penis in hand, staring straight at her.

One weekend they had a party in their house, loads of people, loads of booze, loud music. Later on, as the party wound down and people drifted home, she went to her room and crawled into bed. She woke suddenly, in the early hours, with the curtains flapping in the breeze from an open window and someone's hand between her thighs. As she came to, she thought she recognised the man from across the road, looking down at her. *What is he doing at our party?* she thought. Then, *Oh my god, what is he DOING!*

She leapt up and the man took off, escaping through the open window. Shaking and in tears, she woke one of her housemates, who called the police.

The police didn't take it very seriously, she says. There was a pile of bricks under the window where he had climbed in, but they didn't bother taking fingerprints. We told them about the man across the street, what he did at his window and how

I was pretty sure it was him, but they didn't bother questioning him. They didn't even take down a report. They said, 'Oh, it was probably just someone from the party,' even though they'd seen the pile of bricks under the window. And as if that meant it didn't matter, that it was just some minor incident. Out of everything that happened that night, that was what upset me most, that I couldn't depend on the cops because they didn't care. And one of them was a woman! It was like someone breaking into our house and assaulting me was nothing. I was too scared to sleep in my bedroom after that. It felt like it could happen again at any point and there was nothing I could do about it. I ended up having to move house.

Jesus, someone says, *all these things we go through, especially when we're young. It doesn't bear thinking about, that our daughters, our nieces, our friends' kids might be going through the same thing and be too ashamed to talk about it.*

Someone else tells a story about one particularly traumatic day that had a huge impact on her confidence. She was overseas on a scholarship, staying in student accommodation with lots of other women. The conditions were fairly grim because construction works in the street outside had interrupted the services and they had no running water. This was particularly difficult when the women had their periods; they were having to buy bottled water to keep themselves clean.

I wasn't exactly having a great time there, so I was really excited when my boyfriend told me he was coming to visit, she tells us. *I hadn't seen him for ages because he lived in a different city. I had bought myself a really cute dress, green with white polka dots, so on the day I was going to meet him, I put it on and went to a nearby shopping centre to get my hair done. I had planned on getting a minibus back to the student accommodation before meeting up with him and I was walking to the stop when a man started walking beside me, chatting away about the weather and things.*

Because he seemed fairly inoffensive, and because she wanted to practice speaking the language, my friend spoke back to him as they walked down the stairs and into the underpass that would take her to her stop. When he called her darling and put his arm around her, she knew she'd done the wrong thing. *I was angry about it,* she said, *the way he assumed he had the right to do that, just because I'd spoken to him. I threw his arm off and shouted at him in English, 'Don't fucking touch me!' and I started to walk away, but he came after me and grabbed me round the waist, pulling me backwards. There was a big ticket machine near the wall and I knew he was trying to get me behind the machine and that he was probably going to rape me. I started screaming and kicking but there was no one else in the underpass at that point, no one near enough to help me.*

Fortunately, she was able to break free and although he chased after her when she started to run, he gave up when they got back out into the open where there were more people.

She was badly shaken when she finally got back to the student accommodation, but her overwhelming emotion was one of relief. She had managed to get away relatively unscathed. She had been lucky.

When the time came to go and meet her boyfriend at the bus station, she left the building and tried to cross over the road to get to the bus stop, but because of the road-works and the heavy traffic, it was pretty much impossible. *I kept seeing buses going past but I couldn't get to them,* she said. *Eventually a taxi drove past on my side of the road, and because I was already late I thought I would just get it. I opened the passenger door to ask if he would take me to the bus station, even though it was only five minutes away, and when he agreed I got in.*

They drove along the road for some time and she kept expecting him to turn off towards the station, but he just carried on driving. *Where are you going?* she asked him. *Why don't you turn here?*

The taxi driver made excuses about the roadworks or said he didn't understand her or just didn't answer. By this time my friend was scared and wanted to get out, but she had no idea where she was. They'd been driving for so long that they were now in the middle of nowhere, no houses, no shops, no people, just a big, empty field. The taxi driver pulled over and started making phone calls. *What are you doing, who are you calling? Why aren't you taking me to the station?* she asked, but he just ignored her and made another call.

Eventually he told her she needed to speak to someone, and he handed her his phone. The man on the other end spoke perfect English. *I have some questions for you*, he said. *What are you doing in this country? Are you here alone?*

I was so confused, she says. *I couldn't think straight, had no idea why I was being asked these things or why I was alone in the middle of a field in a taxi. I was yelling into the phone, 'What is going on?' but the guy on the other end just told me to answer the questions. 'I'm here at the university on a scholarship,'* I said, *'and no, I am NOT alone, I'm meeting my boyfriend at the bus station, he'll be waiting there for me now and wondering where I am!'* The man told her she could hand the phone back to the taxi driver.

After speaking to the man on the other end for a few minutes, the taxi driver put down the phone, started the car and turned around, heading back the way they'd come. When they pulled up outside the bus station, he demanded a huge amount of money. *Are you kidding me?* she said. *You've been driving me around for fucking ages, not even going where I wanted to go, and now you're asking me for all this money. I'm not giving it to you.*

The taxi driver got really aggressive, yelling and threatening her, so in the end she handed the money over. As she turned to open the car door, the taxi driver stuck his hand up her skirt and pushed his fingers into her vagina. Gasping with shock, she fumbled with the door handle, managed to get out, and just stood on the pavement yelling at him, *You're an arsehole, you're such an arsehole*, while he laughed at her through the window. When he drove off, she stared after the car, desperately trying to remember the number plate, but she was in too much of a state. The numbers slipped from her brain like coins dropped from a trembling hand. By the time she found her boyfriend in the station, she had forgotten them.

What did you do? we ask. *Did you go to the police? Did you report it?*

No point, she says. *I had no evidence. In any case, it felt like everyone would just think it was my fault for trying to look pretty. Like I had made myself into a beacon for attention and deserved what I got. And so many of the women I knew had been through much worse. There was a German woman who was raped by a gang of young guys at three in the afternoon, down by the river. There were people all around and she was screaming for help, but everyone just ignored her. Afterwards, she literally lost her voice, wouldn't speak to anyone for weeks, she was so traumatised by it. I was quieter too, after I was abused. I didn't ever get dressed up or do my hair again. I tried to stay in the background as much as possible. I didn't want to be noticed.*

She wonders, now, if the man asking her all those questions on the phone was a sex trafficker, trying to assess how vulnerable she was, if she was worth the risk. She considers herself lucky that she wasn't gang raped, sex trafficked or killed. We all think it, that she was lucky she was 'only' assaulted.

———

And so the stories continue. Someone was sexually abused by her GP when she was twelve. Someone else was cornered by a teacher in a cupboard. Every single one of us has at least one story to tell. Most of us are telling stories we haven't told before. Only one of us reported what we experienced to the police. Misogyny has been part of our adolescent landscape, just there in the background, immoveable. Men masturbating in doorways that we walked past, bare breasts and spread thighs splashed across the pages of porn mags that lay scattered like jetsam round the edges of playgrounds, as if washed up on a tide of dirt. I look around the pub and wonder who else is living with these stories inside them. I see the stories stretching out beyond our table, across the city, the country, the globe, multiplying and limitless, like numbers strung along their infinite washing line.

because, globally, 35 per cent of woman have experienced sexual or physical violence at some time in their lives, because an average of 137 women are killed every day by an intimate partner or family member, because less than 40 per cent of women who experience violence look for help, because, of those who do seek help, less than 10 per cent go to the police, because although 155 countries have domestic violence laws and 140 have laws on sexual harassment in the workplace, these laws are not always enforced, because 72 per cent of human-trafficking victims are women or girls, because three out of every four children who are trafficked are girls, because people are mostly trafficked for sexual exploitation, because 200 million women and girls have undergone female genital mutilation, because genital mutilation is physically and mentally traumatic, makes sex very painful and causes long-term health issues, because 15 million adolescent girls have experienced enforced sex, because one in ten women in the EU have experienced cyber-harassment, because 40–60 per cent of women in the Middle East and North Africa have experienced harassment in the street, because 82 per cent of female parliamentarians have experienced psychological violence during their time in office[5]

CHAPTER 16

Resurgence of fear. Writing the book. Different types of stalkers and the importance of sharing stories

When I was in the initial throes of writing this manuscript, friends frequently asked me if it was cathartic and/or traumatic, writing about what I'd gone through. I would look at them quizzically. Cathartic? No. I didn't need to purge myself; it had happened so long ago that I'd already worked through my emotions and had no residual stress to release. It wasn't traumatic either. I was just writing, very matter-of-factly, about what had happened. It wasn't at all like reliving it.

But my blasé attitude changed when I plunged into the murky depths of stalking research. The more I read about other people's experiences, the more I read about how the mind of a stalker worked, the more panicked I became. Had I thought this through properly, or was I just idiotically slogging away at a Project of Doom that was going to rain horror down upon me? The trauma I had been through while actually being stalked began to resurface in cloying waves of panic. What if The Man read the book? How might he react?

In order to answer that question, there were others I needed to ask. What was The Man's motivation for example, what had driven him to pursue me in this way? I knew that individual stalkers had very different motivations, so I browsed the Stalking Risk Profile,[1] trying to work out if any of them fitted The Man. There were five different types of stalker, grouped according to how the stalking began, the motivation and the prior relationship between stalker and target. They were:

1. The Rejected Stalker—stalking begins with the breakdown of a relationship (often a sexual partner but sometimes a family member, close friend or work colleague). The rejected stalker is either looking to reinstate a relationship or to get revenge for a perceived rejection. The stalking can last for a long time because it allows the stalker to carry on feeling close to the victim or makes the stalker feel better about themselves.

2. The Resentful Stalker—stalking begins when the stalker believes they have been mistreated or humiliated and wants revenge. They continue stalking because they gain a sense of power from frightening their victims. Often they feel their behaviour is reasonable because they're fighting back against a perceived injustice.

3. The Intimacy-seeking Stalker—stalking begins with a sense of loneliness and lack of close friendship. Victims are strangers or acquaintances that the stalker fixates on, motivated by the desire for a close relationship. Sometimes the stalker may have delusional beliefs about their victim—for example, believing that they are already in a relationship. They carry on stalking because it makes them feel closely linked to another person.

4. The Incompetent Suitor—again, stalking can begin with a sense of loneliness but might also be motivated by lust. Unlike the person seeking intimacy, however, they are not looking to establish a long-term loving relationship. Instead, they are seeking short-term sexual gratification.

Often the stalking is short lived. When it persists it's because they are unaware or indifferent to the victim's distress, sometimes because of poor social skills or intellectual disability.

5. The Predatory Stalker—stalking begins because of deviant sexual interests. Predators are usually male and their victims female strangers that they have developed a sexual interest in. Stalking is motivated by sexual gratification, the stalker enjoying watching the victim without her knowing, but it might also be used as a way of gathering information in preparation for a sexual assault. They enjoy the sense of power and control that comes from stalking an unsuspecting victim.

I knew The Man hadn't been the 'rejected' or 'resentful' type; those definitions seemed to apply to stalkers who had had a previous relationship with their targets. And the description of the 'incompetent suitor' implied a likelihood of intellectual disability, which didn't fit him either. And although I was sure he had been watching me without me knowing, I didn't think he was preparing for a sexual assault. He had seemed to want contact with me, to establish some kind of relationship. Did that rule out the 'predatory' type?

If so, it left the 'intimacy-seeker'. Maybe he was just someone having a hard time after a divorce, someone who had become confused about boundaries because he was keen to start a new relationship, someone who had now forgotten about me and moved on. Of course, that's what I wanted to believe. But, realistically, nobody ever fits neatly into one 'type' and there are frequently crossovers in stalking typologies. The Man was an individual with a personality and history I knew nothing about. And not knowing him, how could I know what his motivation or his intentions were? All I had to go on was my gut instinct. And my gut had picked up on small clues in every interaction with The Man:

- He had said, 'I'm not trying to find out where you live or anything', a peculiar thing for anyone to say, unless they WERE trying to find out where you lived.

- I had told him I didn't want to meet him for coffee and that I wasn't prepared to give him my email address, yet he had looked up my email address and asked again if I would meet him. Most people would have accepted my refusal and probably would have been embarrassed to pursue things any further. The fact that he was prepared to send me an email when I had told him I didn't think it was appropriate was an indication that he wasn't listening to my 'no'. He was signalling he was the one in control by emailing me anyway, and by repeating the email to me when I told him I hadn't read it.

- He had mentioned the cottage directly opposite my house, alerting me to the fact that he knew where I lived, maybe as a way of making a connection, maybe with the intention of alarming me.

- When he said, *I'll see you later*, the intonation was peculiar, almost threatening. If I told anyone this, it would sound like I had totally lost it, reading threat into such a common phrase, but the spike of alarm it produced in me, the way he had almost sneered as he said it, convinced me there was an element of implied threat there.

- He had used the same phrase I had used when I read poetry at the Big Bike Brekky, and he had mentioned being vegetarian. Again, he might have been trying to establish a connection or he might have wanted me to know he had been following me since that event.

But I didn't know to what extent I could trust my gut instinct when I was in such a state of emotional arousal. When you're suffering from post-traumatic stress, the autonomic nervous system doesn't just react to the sense of immediate danger. It's also responding to internal activity triggered by past life events. My 'truth' was subjective, and I had no way of knowing what The Man's 'truth' was or what previous life events influenced his actions. Perhaps he and his family hadn't been given the help they needed when he was a child. Perhaps he'd been neglected, perhaps he'd never been given autonomy and was now desperately seeking some sense of control and empowerment. Perhaps he was angry at women because of his childhood or adult experiences. Perhaps his ability to frighten me made him feel powerful. But this was all guesswork. I didn't KNOW anything. My friends had been right. There was an element of re-traumatising as I worked through this, and it left me with a horrible catch-22. I wanted to understand what drove people to stalk, because that seemed the only way to find a solution and end the trauma, but looking into it was creating more trauma.

In her extraordinary book *Troll Hunting*,[2] investigative journalist Ginger Gorman sheds new light on the phenomenon of cyberstalking, by actually embedding herself in the world of predator trolls and really listening to their stories in order to work out the source of the problem and understand why these behaviours occur. I asked her how the research had affected her. Did she think the results were worth the trauma?

That is such a hard question, because I'm still recovering from that damage.

I was a mess after writing *Troll Hunting*. I was very alcoholic and I had really bad PTSD and depression as a result of all the relentless violence, misogyny, white supremacy and anti-Semitism. I didn't expect, when I went in, that guys like the Christchurch killer and other kinds of terrorists were the same as predator trolls. No one in the world knew that at the time. Now, since the book came out, it's really become part of the discourse, but it wasn't being talked about in 2018, when I was writing it. So it's a really hard question, because the price

I paid was extreme. It did a lot of damage to me, it did a lot of damage to my family, and I think it was a huge contributor to my marriage falling apart, so it's hard to quantify. I am really proud of the book in the sense that we're seeing lots of policy and attitudinal changes, definitely in Australian society, that can in part be attributed to the work that I did. But I also now have what's basically a chronic illness in terms of PTSD . . . So on a good day, I would say yes, I'm proud of the work we've done, I'm really proud of the way I did it. I think I approached it in a way no one ever had and therefore we got information that we wouldn't get any other way. But would I advise other journalists to do the same? Probably not.

These personal catch-22s reflect a bigger picture. If we want the trauma of gendered abuse to stop, we need to raise awareness. We need statistics to show the extent of misogynistic behaviour and we need to understand why it happens, but the work itself can be traumatising. And if we want to motivate people to work towards change, we need more than facts, figures and explanation. People must feel things if they are to be motivated, and that means sharing stories, which can trigger more abuse from those who would rather we didn't. We only need to look at the experiences of extraordinary women like Brittany Higgins and Grace Tame to see the toll that advocacy can take, particularly when the patriarchy fights back.

This need to narrativise what had happened was something I continually questioned as I wrote the manuscript. Telling the story meant I was forced to choose particular details and leave out others. Sometimes I changed the sequence of events to improve narrative flow. Did this make the story less genuine? The nature of memory is that it becomes less reliable with every telling—how reliable was mine? How accurate was my memory of conversations? Did I really need the story, or would the facts themselves be enough?

Psychologist Robyn Dawes describes humans as 'the primates whose cognitive capacity shuts down in the absence of a story'.[3] Studies have also shown that narrative structure affects our ability to understand and remember a sequence of events and that, when reaching their verdict, juries are heavily influenced by the quality of the defence/prosecution's story.[4] This was all very well, but did it mean I was manipulating readers in the telling of my story?

Tania Lombrozo, psychologist and director of the Concepts and Cognitions Lab at Princeton University, explains why humans rely so heavily on stories.

[Stories and explanations are] two ends of a continuum.

A good story is one that's full of detail and creates visual images and emotions. A good explanation ... might appeal to general features of the world ... [or to] scientific laws or regularities ... Often we do both of these. We do the storytelling, which is very concrete and particular, and we do the explaining, which is much more about extracting the structure of the world in a way that's generalisable. [This helps us to] relate our observations, which are highly variable, changing from moment to moment, to something more like a simple underlying structure that allows us to predict how things might go in the future. It's a way to extract order and regularity from what might otherwise seem disorganised and unsettling.[5]

This is nothing new, of course. Folktales have performed just such a purpose for centuries. The folklorist William Bascom[6] identified that while folktales were certainly told for amusement, they had four further functions:

1. Allowing people to escape from the repressions and demands of their particular society through fantasy.
2. Validating cultural norms and celebrating those who embraced them.
3. Educating children about society's morals and values.
4. Applying social pressure to conform by demonstrating what happened to people who didn't.

Oral folktales originated among peasants, who had little formal education, as a way of presenting life lessons and connecting people to the common values of their particular culture. The stories adapted over time as cultures changed, and gradually disappeared if they became irrelevant. How telling, then, that the tale of Mr Fox, a misogynistic bully who gets his comeuppance thanks to the brave and defiant Mary, fell out of favour, replaced by tales of young ladies who showed their virtue by cooking and cleaning with no word of complaint (Cinderella, Snow White) or doing their father's bidding, however grotesque the request (Beauty and the Beast), while waiting for a prince to rescue them (or their beast to turn into one).

Humans make sense of the world by telling and listening to all sorts of stories. From an evolutionary perspective, we need to hear other people's tales so that we can widen our knowledge and understanding and so keep ourselves safe. The explanations embedded in stories can help us anticipate when things might happen. This is particularly true when people are involved. We want to know who is responsible, who is to blame. Understanding motivation is of particular interest because it can help us to anticipate behaviour patterns and either encourage or prevent them.

However, in the same way that the folktales of old helped to maintain social order by ensuring that the stories told reflected societal values, the patriarchal system has evolved ways of preventing women from telling stories that deviate from patriarchal norms. This is often through the establishment of fear: the fear of not being believed, the fear of incurring wrath, the fear of being branded a harpy, of negative effects on our careers, of being beaten and tortured, of losing our lives. 'Female journalists get silenced all the time,' says Ginger Gorman. 'And this is a very deliberate tactic. It also happens to women in other fields, especially fields that have been traditionally inhabited by men, like sport and politics.' In 2018 Gorman paid the Australian Institute to gather data on cyber-hate. The institute found that 44 per cent of women and 34 per cent of men have been attacked online, but that the *ways* in which women are attacked are significantly different: they are more sexually violent, more extreme and more sustained. I spoke to Ginger about this over the phone. Here's what she said:

It's interesting that whenever we talk about the regulation of the internet in society, people, especially those on the Far Right, throw up their hands and cry, 'Free speech! Free speech is at risk!' but nobody's speech is ever completely free.

There is no situation in real life where it's legal to sexually harass or bully someone at work. There are lots of restrictions on our speech all the time, restrictions around racial hatred and so forth, so it's a nonsense to say that the internet needs to be a place where free speech reigns, because society doesn't operate like that. I think it's fascinating that the people who complain about this the loudest—ultimately white men—are the people whose speech is the most free ... It's people in marginalised groups who get attacked the most. So if you are a woman of colour who is gay and you're loud on the internet, then you will have what I call minority-stacking against you and you're far more likely to be a victim. If you believe in a pluralist society where everyone does have a voice, then these online behaviours have to be stopped. We cannot have an internet which is white supremacist, where those who are marginalised are attacked for speaking out. It's effectively the opposite of free speech, because it silences the voices of those we need to hear the most.

Of course, when women and minorities are too afraid to speak out about abuse, when we only hear the stories that champion fixed-gender roles and assign blame to anyone who subverts them, it's much easier to carry on with the same system and pretend it's all okay. Almost a century ago, W.E.B. Du Bois put this another way in his ground-breaking essay on the importance of listening to black voices: 'All art is propaganda and ever must be, despite the wailing of the purists . . . I do not care a damn for any art that is not used for propaganda. But I do care when propaganda is confined to one side while the other is stripped and silent.'

Growing up

Alex and I are back from London and staying with Alex's parents in Edinburgh. It's not too bad an arrangement. Alex still gets angry sometimes, but living in his parents' house means he has to control his violent outbursts.

His parents seem to like me. In their eyes, I'm 'brainy' (because I'm at university) but not 'up myself' (because I'm a barmaid). I'm also polite and I do things to help out. I notice that Alex's mum, Joan, shoulders pretty much the whole domestic workload, although Alex and I usually do the dishes and manage our own laundry. Alex's dad and brother don't seem to do any housework.

I try to help out by cooking the tea, but I'm a bit nervous about it. Alex's family wouldn't consider a meal without meat to be anything other than a snack, and I'm not used to cooking meat. I shuffle through my memories of the food I was brought up on. I remember corned beef hash was a standby when money was tight. I buy a tin of corned beef, some potatoes and baked beans. I peel and boil the potatoes. There's no potato masher, so I use a fork to make the mash. It takes eons. Eventually I get fed up. I put aside a wee bit for myself, mix the corned beef into what's left and put the dish in the oven. I heat up the beans. When everything's ready we all sit down to eat. Once released from the dish, the grey-potato-plus-pink-meat mess looks like a nasty car accident, the mash is full of hard lumps that the fork missed, and the beans are cold, stuck to the plate with congealed sauce. I look round the table anxiously. Alex's dad, Eddie, lifts a fork to his mouth and shoves the car accident in. He turns his gaze heavenwards, nodding appreciatively, as if his mouth was full of manna.

Mmhmm, he says, *mmhmm. This is brilliant.* He chews and nods, eyes shut in ecstasy, then suddenly his demeanour changes. His eyes ping open and he stabs his fork aggressively at Alex's mother. *How comes YOU don't give us scran like this,* he snaps, *instead of the sloppy shite you usually cook!*

Joan gives him a hard stare but says nothing. I look down at the sloppy shite I'VE just cooked. It feels as if, in attempting to help Joan out, I've unwittingly made things harder for her. I definitely get the impression she likes me a little less right now, and I feel vaguely ashamed, as if I've done something wrong.

———

The following weekend, Eddie asks Alex and I if we'll do a job for him. Alex is wary, but Eddie is offering to pay us £50 each, so we agree. Eddie will be meeting some friends in a pub. We're to arrive half an hour after him. We'll stay for a drink and at some point he'll pass me a package under the table.

Bring your bag with you, he says to me. *It's better if you have the bag, it'll look daft if Alex has one, even if he is a wee poofter, heh-heh. Mind and sit next to me when you come in, and when I pass you the package, put it straight in the bag, alright?*

I nod. My stomach churns. I feel like I'm in a low-budget crime movie and I've been given a part that I'm totally unsuited for.

I'll buy yous a drink when you come in, Eddie says. *Don't go necking them, but soon as yous have finished, say you have to go, right? I'll give yous an address beforehand and that's where you take the parcel.*

If this all sounds a bit dodgy, it's because it is. Eddie is a petty criminal who frequently had long spells in prison when Alex was a child. Mostly his crimes were in the form of mini-heists that he and his colleagues staged on local businesses. Once, they hired a large removal truck and pretended to be clearing out the windows of the Princes Street chain stores in Edinburgh, ready for the new Christmas displays. They cleaned out five or six stores before they were forced to stop because the truck was full. Their families all got great Christmas presents that year, and the people who lived on the local housing estate got some quality goods for knockdown prices.

Eddie prides himself on only stealing from businesses and companies that can afford the loss, but occasionally he has to do time for things he hasn't done. Unable to get them for the window-display scam, the police had instead secured a conviction for a scam on local pensioners. According to Eddie, they were quite open with him about it.

We know this isn't your style, Ed, but we also know about the Princes Street job. You're going to do time for that, one way or another.

This infuriates Alex's dad, who sees himself as a kind of Robin Hood and resents being tarred as someone who would take advantage of the vulnerable, but he seems to accept doing time as an unavoidable pitfall of the job.

We arrive in the pub at the allotted hour. It's mid-afternoon but it's also Saturday, so the pub is full. Most of the clientele are middle-aged men. Eddie and his two mates are sitting in a corner seat near the door. On the table in front of them are three mugs of beer and a big, red McEwan's Export ashtray with three smoking fags balanced on its rim. Eddie waves us across and shuffles round the bench seat to make room for us. As soon as I sit down beside him, he shoves a parcel into my lap.

What are yous having? he asks. Alex asks for a half-and-half (half a pint of lager with a whisky chaser), I ask for a half of cider. Eddie nods at the guy sitting at the other end of the bench seat and he gets up and heads to the bar. I slip the parcel into the bag at my side, then slide the bag onto the floor.

Eddie lifts his fag from the ashtray, inhales, blows the smoke out through his nose. He turns to me. *Good of you to do this, Ellis,* he says. *You're alright, you ken that? Too good for this one, any road.* He jerks his head towards Alex. *If this cunt ever lays a hand on you, you let me ken, I'll sort him out.*

I'm not sure how to respond. I say, *Okay*, and hope that my reply doesn't annoy either Eddie or Alex. I know I'll find out what Alex thinks as soon as we leave the pub.

I have no recollection of where we took the parcel, only that Eddie gave us money to get a taxi there. When we get in the cab, Alex is angry, but thankfully not with me.

Lay a hand on you, he scoffs as we pull away from the kerb. *He's one to fucking talk! I should be sorting HIM out for all HIS laying on of hands. If he wasn't such a fat fucker, that's exactly what I'd do.*

Alex has spoken to me before about his childhood, so I know what he's talking about. When he was wee and his dad was inside, his mum struggled to support the family on her own. She worked in a biscuit factory and their evening meal was often a cup of tea and a plate of broken biscuits. They lived in a first-floor flat on a housing estate in Saughton. After school, or during holidays, the bairns from the estate played together on the patch of green that the blocks of flats surrounded. Tag, Red Rover, rounders, ring-bell-run. When it was time for their tea, a parent (usually a mother) would lean out the window and shout down to the relevant kids that they needed to come home. Alex and his brother and sister would get called in for their tea around the same time but, when they went up the stairs, there was quite often no food for them to eat. Not wanting the neighbours to know she couldn't feed her bairns, his mum called them in for meals that didn't exist.

Things got worse when Eddie was first released from prison. Alex thought his dad probably spent most of his time inside wondering what his mum was getting up to. There was always violence when he first came out. Convinced his wife had been with other men, Eddie would work himself into a fury and beat her up, and if Alex happened to be in the room, he would inevitably end up with a slap or a punch for looking the wrong way, for trying to protect his mother or just for being a 'gawky little poofter'.

Alex has never spoken about this as if it was traumatic, but sitting there in the taxi, listening to him rage about his dad, I realise something for the first time—Alex is depressed. Not that he would admit to that. For Alex, admitting to depression would be like saying, *I'm weak, I'm damaged.* Utterly unthinkable. Yet to me, it's suddenly quite clear. He hates his father for what he did but he's repeating the same pattern with me, which of course means he hates himself. He knows that physical abuse is wrong, because he's witnessed it happening to his mother and felt the horror of it, yet he's been brought up in a culture where men hitting women for imagined infidelities has been accepted, normalised. He must be so confused. What's worse is that his upbringing has also taught him that asking for help is a sign of weakness, that even admitting to having a problem is weak. He has nowhere to turn, so he drinks to dull the pain, maybe even as a form of self-harm.

None of this makes me think Alex's behaviour is okay. I'm still terrified of his anger and angry that he makes me terrified. His upbringing is not an excuse for what he does, but it's certainly a reminder that these behaviours don't come out of nowhere. As Jess Hill points out in *See What You Made Me Do*,[7] 'Most abusive men were once tender little boys, vulnerable and shy, who just wanted to love and be loved. That boy didn't dream about abusing women when he grew up. He didn't dream of becoming a violent father. And yet so many boys grow up to do both.' Women are not the only people who are trained out of responding to their instincts. They're not the only ones who suffer because of gender stereotyping.

because our culture of male entitlement is also unhealthy for men, because men have been taught that they deserve and should expect certain types of behaviour from women, because this makes some men angry when women don't oblige, because men have been taught that their authority is what counts, that this is what will win them respect, because men have been taught that the biggest threat to their authority is their partner having sex with someone else behind their back, because men have been taught that being vulnerable will lose them respect, because this can make it difficult to admit to mistakes or confess to weaknesses, because men have been taught that being sad is weak, that asking for help is weak, that being less knowledgeable is weak, because men have been taught that displays of anger and strength and knowledge are powerful, because men have been taught that, if they want to be attractive to women, they need to display these attributes, when in fact most women would rather they were sensitive and caring, because gender polarity isn't working for anyone

CHAPTER 17

Why is misogyny so persistent? Patriarchal culture

When I was growing up in Britain, patriarchy and feminism were dirty words. They were outdated modes of expression used by unshaved, bra-less hippy women in the sixties and seventies. This was the eighties. We didn't 'let it all hang out' anymore. We were well-groomed power dressers with padded shoulders and big hair. (Though if you were a woman, the 'power' element had to be feminine: cinched waists, lots of pink, bold make-up and high heels.) Women were equal now, the line went, no need for all that 'man-hating'. There was a woman in charge of the country, for heaven's sake, what more did we want? To warn us of what might happen if we tried to get too independent, songs like Hall and Oates' 'Maneater' and The Police's 'Every Breath You Take' were number 1 hits, regularly played on the radio.

It's an ongoing cycle: feminist uprising, backlash, feminist uprising, backlash. It seems whenever there's a real step forward, it's followed by a re-establishment of male authority and sexist values. So why is it so difficult for women to truly be seen as equal? Why, after centuries of protesting, are we still nowhere near gender parity when it comes to wages or positions of power? Why are we still subject to misogynistic abuse and constant, subtle undermining?

In the 'Radically normal' episode of his *The Hidden Brain* podcast,[1] Shankar Vedantam describes an interesting phenomenon. In the States, a 1988 General Social Survey showed that only 11.6 per cent of the population believed that same-sex couples should have the right to marry, which is about as low a percentage as you ever get in a survey of this kind. In 2018 the survey was repeated and the results showed a huge shift in attitude. Sixty-eight per cent supported same-sex marriage. Half the country, tens of millions of people, had changed their opinion. It's almost unheard of for attitudes to change so dramatically in such a short space of time.

Harvard psychologist Mahzarin Banaji observed something similar. Banaji studies implicit bias, the unconscious biases we hold without necessarily being aware of them. Using tests that highlight brain activity when people are shown certain images, she recorded a 33 per cent drop in anti-gay bias in only ten years. If trends like this were to continue, homophobia in the US would be close to non-existent in nine years. By comparison, racism would take another six decades to disappear. And according to the World Economic Forum,[2] current trends suggest that it will be another 208 years before the US closes the pay gap between men and women.

So what had the LGBTQIA+ community got so right? Why had their protests been heard, when the protests of others had fallen on deaf ears? The Stonewall riots that took place in New York in 1969 were a huge turning point, but this doesn't fully explain the dramatic shift in attitudes—there have also been numerous high-profile protests and riots in black communities. Vedantam wondered if it could be the fact that the queer community, or at least the white section of it, was already an integral part of white, middle-class America. As more and more gay people opened up about their sexuality and spoke about the issues they faced, family members, friends and colleagues would frequently change their attitudes. This is different for people of colour, who would not usually be part of white families. However, it doesn't explain the ongoing abuse of, and discrimination against, women, many of whom are intimately connected to white, middle-class America as mothers, daughters, siblings, colleagues and friends.

Gay rights activist Evan Wolfson acknowledges that not all prejudices are the same. 'The stakes involved in entrenched racism, in the entrenched subordination of women, are . . . much greater' he says. In fact, patriarchal/capitalist societies RELY ON the subversion of women and people of colour in order to function. The rights of LGBTQIA+ people can be accommodated without too much disruption to the status quo, but what happens to the economy if women refuse to shoulder the burden of domestic labour, of emotional labour, of childcare and aged care? What happens if women and people of colour are given positions of authority and paid equal wages instead of filling most of the lower-paid, lesser-valued positions?

To understand this, we need to look at the way patriarchy operates. It's important to reiterate here that 'patriarchy' does not equal 'men'. Patriarchy is a system, one that privileges men over women and some men over others. It maintains itself through cultural reinforcement and the policing of behaviour that might upset the status quo. In *The Gender Knot*, Allan Johnson[3] outlines the status quo as defined by patriarchal culture. It is:

1. Male dominated—positions of authority, such as senior politician, head of state, judge, corporate CEO, senior police officer, are usually held by men. Women may occupy these roles, but they will stand out as being an exception and are likely to be heavily judged on their appearance, their reproductive choices and their leadership style (e.g. being labelled 'cold', 'robotic' or 'bitchy' if they are 'too' assertive[4] and weak if they are 'too' willing to negotiate).

2. Male identified—cultural descriptions of masculinity match the core values of society (e.g. 'control, strength, competitiveness, toughness ... logic, forcefulness ... rationality ... control over emotion') while qualities seen as feminine (e.g. 'cooperation, equality ... compassion, caring, vulnerability, a readiness to negotiate and compromise, emotional expressiveness and intuitive ... thinking') are undervalued.

3. Male centred—media and cultural attention is focused on men and boys. Men take centre stage in films, newspaper stories, sports reportage and TV programs. Even when women have central roles (think of those stories we tell our children: Snow White, Sleeping Beauty,

Rapunzel), they're often nothing more than foils for the actions of men.

4. Obsessed with control—any system that favours one group of people over another relies on control. Men, particularly white middle-class men, maintain their privilege by controlling women *and* other men, especially those who don't adhere to patriarchal standards. If a man displays any qualities deemed feminine (compassion, vulnerability, emotional expression), he will pay dearly for it. Men must be seen to be constantly in control, cool, unemotional (except when angry or enraged), knowledgeable and commanding, especially in their interactions with women.

These four pillars of patriarchy support the overarching ceiling of entitlement that protects the system. If men are assigned very specific modes of behaviour and ways of being, and those behaviours are seen as synonymous with leadership roles, then of course men will feel entitled to hold those positions. Women who somehow manage to achieve a leadership role will be viewed with suspicion, and some men will feel entitled to undermine them at every turn, justifying their behaviour with phrases like, *If you can't stand the heat, keep out of the kitchen* or *It's just a bit of banter, lighten up.* If the cultural focus is always on the actions and achievements of men, reinforcing the value of those 'masculine' traits and the importance of men's lives over and above the lives of others, then men will feel entitled to respect and adoration from those who are not men.

In her book *Entitled*,[5] Kate Manne argues that, rather than focusing on individual perpetrators, 'it is best to think of misogyny primarily as a property of the social environments girls and women navigate, wherein they are liable to be subject to hateful or hostile treatment because of their gender'. Misogyny isn't necessarily the hatred of women, she argues. Instead, it can be understood as patriarchy's police force, working to ensure that gendered norms are adhered to. Sexism, on the other hand, is the theoretical branch of the patriarchal system, 'the beliefs, ideas and assumptions that serve to rationalize . . . patriarchal norms . . . including gendered division of labour and men's dominance over women in areas of traditionally male power'.

Yes, things have changed a lot over the years, but many men and boys are still unconsciously learning that it's the woman's role to give (sex, emotional support, childcare, domestic labour) and the man's role to take (sex whenever desired, emotional support, leisure time/career pursuit while the other work is being done). The messages are rarely voiced loudly (though sometimes they are). Mostly, the system operates on a more covert level, delivering its message in subtler ways. It's a culture that easily accommodates, and may even encourage, stalking behaviour.

That's not to say that entitlement necessarily leads to stalking. As detailed in chapter 12, stalking involves a wide range of behaviours and motivations, some of which may begin with parental neglect or abandonment in childhood. Denied access to a nurturing caregiver, children grow up with a fear of being unloved, maybe even unlovable. As adults, they enter a society that gives greater status to those with the power to attract adoration and receive sexual gratification, and they feel left out. Add to that a system that reinforces men's rights over and above women's, that tells men they have the *right* to sex, the *right* to power, the *right* to respect, and you can see how a male stalker might easily find a way to justify his desperate behaviour to himself. But that's not the whole story.

I spoke again to Ann Moulds, CEO of Action Against Stalking. Ann recognises the impact of living in a patriarchal society and the sense of entitlement that can enable a stalking mentality, but she points out the importance of looking beyond that. 'Not all stalking is gender-based violence,' she tells me. 'We need to remember that women sometimes stalk men, there's same-sex stalking, and child abduction and human trafficking also involves stalking. In order to best help victims, we need to look at individual cases and try to work out the stalker's motivation, because that has an impact on how to deal with the behaviour.'

What's also important to recognise is that while this system has evolved as a way of keeping women in their place, it places huge demands on men too. 'As a group, men are dominant and privileged in relation to women,' writes

Jess Hill.[6] 'But as individuals, men pay a price for this privilege: to be considered "real men", they have to live up to patriarchy's standards and abide by . . . rules (that) are regulated—through fear, control and violence—by other men.'

My son, an easy-going, confident and popular teenager, would occasionally have days where he couldn't face going to school. When I asked what the problem was, he would sigh heavily and tell me it was just hard being judged all the time. Constantly surrounded by large groups of (mostly) males, the pressure to conform was enormous, with behaviour carefully policed. Anything that bucked stereotypical male norms was immediately called out. In fact, competitiveness and one-upmanship was so high that any minor point of difference or slip of the tongue would be jumped on. Even having the wrong thing in your lunch box could spark name calling and derision. Add this to the high academic demands of school and it's no wonder that so many of our boys and young men are depressed.

In his Australian TV series *Man Up*,[7] Gus Worland found that the problem doesn't disappear when boys leave school. By talking to men and boys across the country, Worland discovered that while men are encouraged to do things together and look out for each other, this isn't happening when it comes to feelings of depression. Men are wary of talking about depression for fear of being seen as weak and pathetic, or being criticised for putting a downer on things. This is particularly true for men who work in male-dominated environments such as construction, which has a higher rate of suicide than any other occupation. A culture of machismo and stoicism means men are bottling their emotions, which leaves them feeling alone and helpless in a cultural landscape where asking for help doesn't seem to be an option. They don't feel dominant or empowered, they feel overwhelmed. Inevitably this can lead to explosions of anger and violence. Or suicide.

Of course, the fact that this is an entrenched cultural problem is not an excuse for individuals who engage in deeply misogynistic behaviour. As adults, we have to take responsibility for our actions and there's no excuse for anyone committing physical or psychological violence against others. It's important to call out horrific acts of misogyny: rape, gendered violence, psychological abuse, stalking. But we must also be aware of misogyny's more clandestine operations and realise that the ongoing sense of being undervalued, silenced, disrespected, treated as an object of desire or derided if not deemed attractive enough deeply affects women's lives. And to realise, also, that men behaving badly are not necessarily 'scary monsters and supercreeps', but people caught in a system that's using them to perpetuate its own belief structure.

There's a lot of misogynistic messaging that goes under the radar. Patriarchal culture encourages ways of thinking and ways of speaking that undermine women so subtly that men AND women unconsciously participate in it. The following conversation with my partner (a strong ally, who is very conscious of patriarchal misogyny and social injustice) is an example.

We were building a pergola in our backyard. One half was to be used for outdoor dining, the other half for a firepit. My partner had seen a problem in the design: he was keen to keep the structure symmetrical but it was quite difficult because of the different proportions of the two areas.

I got out the plans I had drawn up and suggested moving a couple of posts and rejigging the layout.

Hang on, my partner said. *I think I need to draw this out separately so I can understand it.* He grabbed a bit of paper and, with my help, did a quick sketch of the layout I was describing. *Okay*, he said, *what I suggest is . . .* and he reiterated the suggestion I had just made.

I turned to look out the window, quietly sighing like Oliver Hardy turning to the camera when Stan has messed up again. I was thinking of Nina Eliasoph's study[8] of language and gender, how men are brought up to communicate in ways that maintain their authority, but I didn't point any of this out to my partner. I didn't want to offend or undermine him. Instead, I seethed inwardly. Of course, my partner, who has lived with me for over twenty years, knew something was up.

What is it? he asked. *You're looking away as if I've said something stupid.*

It's just because you're telling me something that I told YOU five minutes ago, I muttered a little sheepishly.

I don't understand what's wrong, he said. *I'm just trying to think this through, so I'm kind of explaining it to myself.*

But you said, 'What I suggest is . . .' I said, *and it wasn't your suggestion, it was mine.*

Right. So how do I say that so it's not offensive?

How about, 'I liked your suggestion that . . .'

Oh, okay. So, I liked your suggestion that we move these posts over there . . .

We've been through this, or something similar, on a number of occasions. These things take time to mend. There's a whole lifetime of culture and upbringing to undo, for both of us. Female and male brains may not be biologically different but their neural pathways have been moulded differently. I've unconsciously accepted that the male ego is a fragile beast that has to be nurtured. And, not wanting to offend the beast, I wouldn't have bothered confronting my partner about owning my suggestion until fairly recently. Instead, I would have shrugged off his question, saying it was fine, there was nothing wrong. Post #MeToo, my consciousness has been raised enough to realise these patriarchal habits NEED to be called out if anything is to change.

My own behaviour needs to change, too. I'm still working on over-apologising, on taking responsibility for other people's happiness, on being afraid to speak out about discrimination, on body-shaming myself, on judging other women and men based on learnt assumptions about how they should behave. I can see that, like me, my partner is trying. He doesn't want to be sexist. He doesn't want to undermine me. When he does, it's because he isn't aware he's doing it.

I imagine it's the same for most men and, indeed, most women. We're so indoctrinated, it's just our normal. It's hard to stop thinking the way we've always thought, to stop speaking the way we've always spoken. We all need accountability, reminders, a willingness to change. We're all tattooed slaves with secret messages beneath our hair, and even if we've shaved our heads so that we can see the messages, getting rid of them is much harder.

Walking alone at night

It's several years since I've seen The Man and I think I'm over it. I'm no longer fearful of going anywhere alone, I no longer feel the need to move among crowds.

On this particular night, I've been to a poetry reading and I'm heading home via public transport. When I get off at my stop, I have a ten-minute walk to get home, but that's fine, I'm okay with that, even though it's dark and the street is deserted. Totally deserted. No one to be seen anywhere. No one no one no one no one. Puddles of light at the foot of each streetlamp, but deeper waters of dark in between.

I rummage in my bag for my keys and hold them inside my pocket, forefinger stretched along the length of one as if it's a knife. As I get closer to my street, I see the dark shape of a man in the distance. I can't tell if he's coming towards me or walking away. I grip my keys tighter in my fist. As I get closer, I realise he's walking in the same direction as me, but he's very slow and his movements are erratic, his body swaying from side to side. I can hear him mumbling to himself. I slow down, figuring he's either drunk or on drugs, or maybe has some kind of personality disorder. Unpredictable. Scary. I dawdle behind him, not wanting to get too close.

Eventually I get frustrated about having to walk so slowly and decide to cross the road instead. I pick up speed until I'm past him on the opposite pavement, then I sneak a quick look back.

What I see makes my fingers relax their grip on the keys,

and my mouth relax into a smile. I nearly burst out laughing. What an idiot I am!

In his book *Blink*,[9] Malcolm Gladwell points out something similar to Joel Pearson's findings detailed in chapter 9: first impressions are not always as intuitive as we think they are. We often make snap judgements about people based on our own unconscious biases. Sometimes what we think of as gut instinct can be an apprehension based on prejudice. De Becker sees things differently.[10] He says that intuition is always right, even when it's wrong. I decide that both Gladwell and de Becker have good points to make. I've made a snap judgement about the man on the other side of the street, one that is prejudiced by my experience with The Man and by the stories I've been told about women being attacked in the street. Nonetheless, these attacks do happen and I was right to be wary, even though, in this case, I wasn't in any danger.

Now that I'm ahead of him, I can see the man has a baby in a carrier on his chest. I can see the tiny arms and legs, the wee feet bouncing against the man's stomach as he walks. I can hear that he's not mumbling to himself, he's singing to the baby, rocking it with the swaying motion of his body.

I get a rush of nostalgia for those days when my own bairns were wee, the hours I and my partner spent pounding the streets at night, trying to get them off to sleep. I feel a sudden warmth towards this man who is starting out on his parenthood journey. He's no longer a demon, a monster preparing to attack. Now I can see him clearly, I realise he's not that different to me.

because there are many men out there trying to do the right thing, to be good parents, to be good partners, to be good people, because the problem is not men as a whole but The Man, the system that stalks all of us, insinuating itself into our lives, our brains, because it leaves its messages tattooed on our scalps, because it makes us all fearful, afraid to express ourselves, afraid to trust our instincts, afraid to show the many different sides of our wonderful, complex selves

CHAPTER 18

Changing our thinking. The importance of collaboration

Those messages on our scalps might be difficult to shift, but that's not to say we can't do it. Social evolution tells us that societies get better over time: more tolerant, more inclusive, more aware of issues of social justice and equality. Slavery was abolished, women were given the vote, homosexuality was decriminalised, apartheid dismantled and segregation stopped because people were angry enough to fight for change and to call out injustice, even when it was dangerous to do so. And it wasn't just those who were directly affected who fought for the changes. Men joined the fight for women's suffrage, white people fought for the abolition of slavery, heterosexual allies fought for the decriminalisation of homosexuality. Change involves listening to the stories of others and fighting alongside them for what's right, as Lady Mary's brothers and friends did, making sure Mr Fox could no longer carry out his grisly deeds.

There's a great deal still to fight for. When I started writing this book, Trump's rise to power had made abundantly clear the underlying racism, sexism, homophobia and transphobia that was, and still is, rife in the US. Trump had tickled the beast of America and it had rolled over and shown its underbelly, but he couldn't stop social evolution. In fact, he was, inadvertently, a catalyst for change. There was a huge backlash against what Trump revealed. Horrified at the mud and gunk sticking to the underside of the beast, all around the world people became louder about equality, diversity and inclusivity. The rise of the #MeToo and Black Lives Matter movements led to better awareness of systemic misogyny and racism throughout the Western world and beyond, and a greater willingness to combat it.

This was particularly evident in the media, a current mechanism for storytelling. There was a huge increase in the publicity of women's sport, with many matches being televised. Female film directors and screenwriters were also being celebrated, alongside Black Lives Matter films and films relating to LGBTQIA+ rights. More women and people of colour began to appear on, and host, quiz and panel shows (though there's still a long way to go before we reach parity). Even advertising changed, featuring greater numbers of people of colour and same-sex couples, showing women driving cars for thrill and adventure (not just to get the shopping or pick the kids up from school) and men engaged in domestic routines like doing the laundry or changing nappies. Nando's 'Everyone is Welcome' campaign (released around the time of the 2017 inauguration and highlighting the company's commitment to employing immigrants, opposing racism and respecting people's religious, sexual and cultural differences) went viral on social media and boosted sales by 122 per cent.[1]

By the time I came to the end of my first draft of the book, bigger changes were afoot. I wrote this final chapter sitting outside the same café I once saw The Man sitting in. After years of avoiding the place, I was at last able to relax there, sipping latte and happily tapping at my keyboard without constantly looking over my shoulder, worried he might suddenly appear. Cars, buses, delivery vans and motorbikes honked and growled their way along the busy street, but somewhere behind the noise of the traffic a blackbird was singing. After several grey-cloud, cold-wind days, the sky was now paintbox blue, and ponytails of sunlight swung around the tables.

The world was sunnier in other ways too. That morning, Joe Biden had won the state of Pennsylvania, giving him enough electoral college votes to claim victory in the election and become the president-elect of the United States. Kamala Harris would become the first female vice president. 'While I may be the first woman in this office,' Harris said, 'I will not be the last, because every little girl watching tonight sees that this is a country of possibilities.'[2]

Biden's victory speech called for an end to 'this grim era of demonisation':[3] 'We are seeing . . . across the world, an outpouring of joy, of hope, renewed faith in tomorrow to bring a better day,' he said. 'I pledge to be a president who seeks not to divide but to unify . . . It's time to put away the harsh rhetoric, to lower the temperature, see each other again, listen to each other again. And to make progress, we have to stop treating our opponents as enemies . . . This is a time to heal . . . marshal the forces of decency, the forces of fairness . . . the forces of science and the forces of hope.'

From my position of privilege on a different continent, Biden's speech was like a cloud that had burst and released sweet rain over a bushfire. His rhetoric was the antithesis of Trump's and it felt like something the world needed to hear. But I could also see that this message of unity would be difficult for people who had been directly impacted by Trump's governance: people of colour, people with disabilities, the LGBTQIA+ community, people who had been affected by COVID-19, people living below the poverty line, people who cared about the environment, people who weren't Republican heterosexual, white males. After four years of being disrespected, discounted, hearing the president condone (or indeed deliver) verbal and physical attacks on you, or dismiss the disease that is killing you or a loved one as nothing more than a bad flu, how could you be anything other than angry, how could you even begin to think about Trump and his supporters as anything other than opponents?

Anger, as we've seen, has its place when it comes to instigating change. It can bring marginalised communities together to fight a common cause. It can be the fuel for social movements like the Arab Spring, #MeToo and Black Lives Matter. It can give a voice to people who have been silenced, as the recent exposé of misogynistic culture in Australia's Parliament House has shown, and it can draw attention to important issues. Anger is necessary, but anger alone doesn't often lead to long-term change. It's good for galvanising like-minded people into action and raising awareness, but not so great when it comes to persuading opponents to think differently.

In his book *Conflicted*, Ian Leslie explains why.[4] When we hear someone loudly voicing an opinion that is in direct opposition to our own, our brains are flooded with chemical signals that tell us we're under attack. This puts us on the defensive and stimulates either our fight or our flight responses—we become aggressive and lash out, or we back off, hoping to avoid conflict. Neither response is conducive to working towards change.

While conflict is essential to evolution, Leslie argues, it's important to disagree in the right way. We need to connect with our opponents, establishing a relationship of trust. We need to stop trying to control what the other person thinks or feels. We need to take opportunities to make the other person feel good about themselves and to be interested in what they're saying, rather than trying to undermine them in an effort to win the argument. We need to apologise when we're wrong, because admitting to error can help strengthen the relationship. Most importantly, we need to 'make an honest human connection'. Leslie is careful to recognise that none of this is easy—we're fighting against a basic biological response. But it's something we can get better at with practise.

It's an approach that Ginger Gorman instinctively took when writing *Troll Hunting*.[5] During our phone call she tells me:

When it comes to trying to stop predator trolling, you've got to go right to the root of it.

You have to pull the weed out by the roots, and that means asking why is this happening, who are these people, what are their motivations? [I didn't realise at the time, but] people later told me I had used radical empathy when I was researching *Troll Hunting*. I didn't know what that was, so I googled it and I found out it's a way of approaching other people, also known as unconditional positive regard, where you assume the best of someone rather than the worst. You go in, not trying to change your own mind, but just really listening. So that's what I did with the predator trolls, and I think because of that, we got the answers that we wouldn't have got any other way.

So if you ask me why these angry young men are behaving like this, I can answer that question because of using unconditional positive regard. And the answer is that from when they were tiny little boys, basically, they have been completely unparented. They've had no humans around. They come from violent, damaged homes and they've been left alone on the internet, where they've imbibed these radical ideologies—white suprem-acy and misogyny—and they've been spat out the other end as radicalised predator trolls and, in some cases, terrorists. I think that's really useful for us to understand, because if we know that these little boys are getting radi-calised and damaged in this way, and harming others later, then we've got a chance of stopping it.

If we're not willing to go in and listen to each other and find the source of the problems and understand why and how things are happening, we're never going to solve society's ills and this will continue. If we took the time to engage with these blokes, would they be so angry, would they do the damage they do? I don't think they would, that's my experience. I've sat embedded with these guys, and a lot of them, not all of them but quite a number of them, changed their behaviour in the process.

In her TED talk, justice-reform activist Nisha Anand[6] also talks about working with people whose ideologies are directly opposed to her own. She wanted to reform the 'Tough on Crime' criminal justice system, a system that she believed discriminated against people of colour and those living in poverty, and one that had led to prisons bursting at the seams with people who had committed minor crimes. But she couldn't make those reforms without the backing of some Republican senators, so she tried to think of ways that she could convince them that what she was arguing for was right.

She appealed to the fiscal conservatives by emphasising that the system was costing taxpayers a huge amount of money and wasn't getting results, was in fact creating a bigger problem. She appealed to the libertarian right, who believed in less government, by demonstrating that the system was an expansion of government control and police powers. She appealed to the religious right by talking about second chances and redemption, values that were missing from the 'Tough on Crime' agenda. They managed to form a bipartisan coalition that passed a reform act and gave seven thousand people a significant reduction in their sentences. As a result, many were immediately released and the prison system became easier to manage. Anand believes that change on a large scale needs large movements, and that searching for common ground, finding a shared humanity with the opposition, is imperative if your movement is to grow.

Another TED talk, by communications expert Howard Rheingold,[7] debunks the myth that success is all about winning and that businesses, political parties and nations only succeed by defeating and dominating the competition. Rheingold sees a different story, one in which cooperation, interaction and interdependency play an important role. He points out that evolution has always relied on collective action. Prehistoric humans had to form alliances with neighbouring tribes with whom they had had disagreements, so they could work together to hunt for food instead of fighting with each other. The development of the alphabet, and later the printing press, enabled millions of people to become literate and thereby communicate across greater distances, so that knowledge was shared and new forms of collective action evolved. Nowadays, the internet allows every desktop to be a printing press, a broadcasting station or a marketplace. Evolution is speeding up as more and more ideas are shared with wider and wider audiences. By listening to each other and sharing thoughts, we're getting cleverer quicker, we're solving more problems and our lives, on the whole, are getting better. Collaboration is key.

In her 2020 speech on the International Day for the Elimination of Violence against Women, the executive director of UN Women, Phumzile Mlambo-Ngcuka, also called for collaboration.[8] She cites the cooperation of scientists, governments, society and industry as a 'game-changer' in the COVID-19 pandemic, and she tries to imagine a world where similar levels of expertise, funding and energy were invested to stem the surge of violence against women.

In 2019, 243 million women and girls, worldwide, were sexually or physically violated by their partners.[9] Mlambo-Ngcuka suggests that collaboration on a grand scale, between governments, the judiciary, the police force, activists, women's organisations, crisis centres, helplines etc., is imperative if this is to change. Cultural change is also required, of course. We need to stop shaming the survivors of abuse. We need to stop normalising the behaviour of the perpetrators. Society needs to encourage men not to be violent and to hold them accountable if they are. And importantly, says Mlambo-Ngcuka, we need to engage men and boys in the fight.

This is already happening. Alongside Elizabeth Nyamayaro, Mlambo-Ngcuka set up the United Nations HeForShe movement, which invites men and boys around the world to stand alongside women and create a shared vision of gender equality. They are aiming for tangible systemic change, but they know that they need to get men onside for that to happen. They're asking men and boys to be accountable for their own actions, but they're also asking universities and businesses to change their policies so that gender equality can flourish.

Here in Australia, in 2010, the Male Champions of Change was set up to encourage men in leadership roles to step up beside women in the fight for change. Elizabeth Broderick, founder of MCC, says the organisation began when women working for change realised that men were missing from the picture and that they had a really important role to play.[10] Currently men dominate Australian industries, so if change is going to happen, particularly in the workplace, it needs decent men in positions of power to spruik gender equality to other men.

Initially the organisation aimed to make the wider population aware of gender equality issues, but today their remit is more about actively finding ways to redress the balance. Alan Joyce, CEO of Qantas, says that there are now clear targets, guidelines on how to work towards those targets and a determination to achieve them. Andy Vesey, managing director of AGL, talks about the 'leadership shadow', the importance of leading by example in the way you talk, the things you do and in holding yourself accountable. Working with groups such as Women's Leadership Institute Australia, the Diversity Council Australia and the Workplace Gender Equality Agency, MCC organisations have been inspired to take action, making their roles flexible, dismantling barriers for carers, responding to domestic and family violence and insisting on 50/50 shortlists for job interviews. There's much still to be done, but as more companies join and more leaders take up the fight, the rate of change is accelerating and gender parity within industry is beginning to look like a real possibility. As the Equal Opportunities Commission commented in their review of the South Australian police force,[11] 'An organisational culture in which gender equality is simply part of how business is done, and how people work together, is not just important for human rights and equal opportunity but is essential for high performance. Mounting global research shows that an increase in gender equality, particularly at leadership levels, has a positive impact on organisational capability and operational effectiveness.'

These organisations are, consciously or otherwise, adopting the social connection model developed by political theorist Iris Marion Young.[12] Young's theory claims that, while individuals may not be to blame for structural injustice (sweatshop labour, for example), those 'connected' to the injustice (e.g. those who buy clothes produced in sweatshops) share some of the burden of responsibility for affecting structural change. (They may choose NOT to buy clothes produced in this way, or they might lobby companies to change their practice.) The model recognises that individuals make a huge number of choices based on circumstances and systems that they live within and, while they shouldn't be blamed or punished for this, it can still be appropriate for them to contribute to repairing the harm. Large scale problems need to be tackled by large scale movements, and it's much easier to get lots of people involved in solutions when we focus on working together rather than apportioning blame.

Collaborative work is also being done in the arena of stalking. I spoke via Skype with Associate Professor of Criminology Susanne Strand at Örebro University, Sweden, about RISKSAM, a research project that is looking into the best structure for a collaborative approach to preventing stalking and intimate partner violence.

It's important to collaborate in any cases of IPV, but particularly for stalking, since stalking per se is a series of repeated crimes.

We know that perpetrators commit several different types of actions—some of them might be defined as crimes by law, others might not—but for the victims, a crime is being committed 24/7 and everyone needs to keep that in mind. The knowledge about stalking is not great in any single organisation, so meeting and collaborating between organisations will increase the knowledge and make it easier to monitor ongoing actions, because we know there is a high level of recidivism in stalking cases.

The RISKSAM meetings would mainly involve social services and the police, because in Sweden they are in charge of the majority of protective actions that can be suggested to victims. In most countries you have to report a crime to receive help from crime prevention, so in the case of stalking, if the victim reports the behaviours and keeps getting the same response over and over—'We can't do anything. That isn't a crime. We don't know who it is'—then they'll stop reporting. With RISKSAM, you're not having to report to the police, you're reporting to social services and getting help from them, and I think if things can be simultaneously pursued through avenues other than criminal justice, crime prevention might work better.

I asked if any other organisations might be involved in these meetings.

The idea is to support the victims and help them to cope so health agencies that might be able to help with that could be included. And, of course, the main objective should be to stop the stalking, so district attorneys might also be part of the meeting because in Sweden they are in charge of restraining orders. Restraining orders can be useful in protecting the victim, but they need to be followed up, and every breach needs to go to court, which is currently not the case anywhere in the world. However, if we increase collaboration there might be a better understanding of why restraining orders are so important in stalking cases.

I asked Dr Strand why she thought that successful risk management of stalkers was so low, when recidivism and the risk factors associated with mental health problems were so high.

Currently, the risk management toolbox overall is very, very small.

There needs to be more knowledge of stalking and more creativity of thinking so that a greater variety of risk management strategies can be applied. One of the reasons this is so difficult when it comes to stalking is because the actions of the stalker might not be illegal per se. It's not illegal to wait outside a person's work or outside a store but, of course, for the victim that doesn't matter. It's a threat every time the stalker appears around you. This is why society has such difficulty handling stalkers, because you need to have a good reason for putting a restraining order on someone, and in many countries that reason has to be that the person has committed a crime. So if, for example, we are trying to categorise the stalking as harassment, instead of looking at each action individually and asking if it's a crime or not, we need to look at all the actions together. It IS harassment if a person is standing outside your work every day; even if the stalker doesn't say anything, doesn't do anything, just standing there every day is harassment. But currently not by law. That's something that needs to be debated.

Did she feel that treating the stalkers might also be a valuable part of managing the risk?

I'm a criminologist but I'm also trained in research psychology, so to put these things together, yes, stalkers also need to be given more help. If a person has continued stalking for more than a year, then that tells us that this person has difficulty letting go and that either they don't understand the problems they are causing their victims, or they do understand it and that is the point of the stalking. Then, of course, they need help managing that and a mental health centre may be able to give them that help.

However, while mental health agencies might be involved in treating someone with stalking issues, they wouldn't usually be involved in helping to stop the stalking as things stand at the moment. The problem with collaboration is that often you're not allowed to share all kinds of information. But you ARE allowed to share risk assessment without going into detail, so if, for example, you're at a RISKSAM meeting and social services say, 'We think this person is a moderate risk,' and the police say, 'We think they're low risk,' and then mental health services say, 'Oh no, this is definitely a high risk situation,' then that could be enough for the other parties to say, 'Okay, if mental health assess this as high risk of recidivism, then we have to trust them, and trust that they will put in the risk management that they think is appropriate. So what do WE need to do to support that?' There are ways of sharing without telling everything.

And what about those young children, neglected or abandoned by parents? Is there a way of addressing these problems early on, as Bessel van der Kolk suggested in chapter 14? Well, if we recognise that the brain is a plastic thing, in a constant state of learning and changing according to experience, we must also recognise that it's possible to prevent anti-social behaviours by nurturing children.

Beginning in the mid-1970s, David Olds and his colleagues developed a program in the US for early intervention that they hoped would eventually lead to a reduction in the development of serious anti-social behaviours in adulthood. After more than twenty years of extensive research, they created the Prenatal and Early Childhood Nurse Home Visitation Program to help low-income, first-time parents start productive lives with their children.[13] Nurses visited mothers while they were pregnant, helping them to improve health through diet as well as by stopping or cutting back on smoking, drinking and substance abuse. This helped reduce the chances of children being born with neurological problems. The visits continued weekly or fortnightly for the first two years of the children's lives. During this time, parents learnt positive childcare practices: how to establish a nurturing and safe home environment, consistent discipline and good health care for children. Nurses also spoke to parents about practising birth control, planning future pregnancies, reaching their educational goals and finding adequate employment. The results were extraordinary. They found that:

1. Three- and four-year-old children of women who did not receive a nurse home visitor, and who smoked ten or more cigarettes per day during pregnancy, had impaired intellectual functioning. The mothers also reported far more fussiness and irritability in their babies. However, children of mothers who were smoking ten or more cigarettes when they signed up for the program but received a nurse home visitor who helped them to cut down on cigarettes were NOT intellectually impaired, and the mothers reported far less fussiness and irritability.[14] The findings suggest that the guidance mothers received from their nurse home visitors not only helped them cut down or stop smoking, it also improved their infants' soothability, which made infant care much easier.

2. For children from birth through to age fifteen, the program reduced state-verified cases of child abuse and

neglect by 79 per cent.[15] In the second year of life (age thirteen to 24 months), nurse-visited children had 56 per cent fewer visits to an emergency room for injuries and ingestions than children not receiving home visits by nurses.[16] During the two-year period after the program ended (from the second through to the fourth year of life), children from nurse-visited families were 40 per cent less likely to be seen in a physician's office for injuries, ingestions or social problems, and they had 35 per cent fewer visits to the emergency room.

3. In a fifteen-year follow up of the nurse home-visitation program,[17] the long-term effects of the program on children's criminal and antisocial behaviour were substantial and had ground-breaking implications for juvenile justice and delinquency prevention. Adolescents whose mothers received nurse home-visitation services over a decade earlier were 60 per cent less likely than adolescents whose mothers had not received a nurse home visitor to have run away from home, 55 per cent less likely to have been arrested, and 80 per cent less likely to have been convicted of a crime.[18] They also smoked fewer cigarettes per day, had consumed less alcohol in the past six months, and had exhibited fewer behavioural problems related to alcohol and drug use.

It's incredibly encouraging to note that this type of intervention can enable families to get a stronger start and children to develop into healthier, happier adults. Of course, the approach taken by the nurses involved in the program was key to its success, with unconditional positive regard a major factor in the nurses' ability to work effectively with members of the group and achieve such great results. Speaking out about problems, collaboration between groups, finding solutions by listening to different opinions and making an 'honest human connection' with others are all necessary if real change is to happen.

———

If this was an old folktale, we would now have come to the end. Mary would have told her story publicly and Mr Fox would have been brought to justice. But it's not a folktale and it's not the end. We've a long way to go yet. The future, at least in terms of social evolution, is looking brighter than the past, and I have no doubt that fewer women, girls, trans and non-binary people will have to put up with the things my generation were forced to put up with. Things WILL change, but if we don't want to wait another 208 years for gender equality we need to step up.

because gendered violence against women is still a thing, because female genital mutilation is still a thing, because rape is still a thing, because sexual harassment in the workplace is still a thing, because so-called 'honour killings' are still a thing, because gender stereotyping is still a thing, because female infanticide is still a thing, because intimate partner violence and coercive control is still a thing, because discrimination is still a thing, because stalking is still a thing, because the most shocking thing about everything I've told you is that none of it is unusual or extraordinary, because this is what an ordinary life looks like for a woman, because it's far worse for trans or non-binary people and for women who identify as part of other minority groups, because this is a problem that everyone has to address if we want to live in a fair and equal society

Regarding the future

My son has just come home from school. I hear the thump as he drops the enormously heavy bag he has to carry to and from the establishment onto his bedroom floor, then the scuffling sounds of him shedding his uniform. Eventually he comes through to the kitchen with his school laptop under his arm.

Mum, he says, *do you have time to watch a video with me? It's just a short one.*

We sit down together on the sofa. *It's about women in sport,* he says. *People at school were talking about it and I want to know what you think.*

The video he shows me is Ben Shapiro slating Nike's new 'Dream Crazier' ad,[19] which celebrates women's achievements in sport and points out some of the barriers women have had to face. Shapiro argues that prominent female athletes are not victims because they're earning millions of dollars (as if wealth were a barrier to discrimination) and that women in general currently have better lives than anyone else on the planet. (What, ALL women? Even the genitally mutilated, the sexually abused, those living with intimate partner violence? Are women really leading better lives than men?) However, he also makes a valid point about the irony of Nike using women's rights to sell trainers, given their poor human rights history.

What did YOU think about it, I ask my son.

I'm not sure, he says. *Some of what he's saying doesn't sound right, but then he's also making some good points and backing them up with evidence. It's a bit confusing.*

I tell him it's difficult, deciding what's right, that people can be very persuasive, especially if they feel strongly about something. I tell him that I think what Shapiro is saying to back up his statements is opinion rather than evidence. In his opinion, women are only described as hysterical when they're actually hysterical, the same way that men are. In his opinion, no one has ever said there's something wrong with wearing a hijab when you're playing a sport. But he's clearly not an expert on women's rights or gender equality. It doesn't even sound like he's done much research on it. And if women in sport are saying they're experiencing discrimination, or if women in general are saying they're described as hysterical whenever they get angry, it's not his place to say, 'No, you aren't.' How would he know?

We chat about it a bit more, then my son gets up to go. He stops in the kitchen doorway and turns back to me. *Thanks, Mum*, he says.

I don't know what the outcome of our conversation was, but knowing my son, I wouldn't be surprised if he took it back to his friends in school the next day, made the same point to them. Young people have so much to deal with in this quickly evolving world, but the more I see and hear from them, the greater hope I have for the future. Most of the young people I speak to are far more accepting of cultural, sexual and physical diversity than their adult counterparts. They ask questions about what they see and hear. And, most importantly, they listen to the answers.

Notes

Why this book

1. Philip Graham, 'The Shadow Knows', *Assay: A Journal of Non-fiction Studies*, vol. 5, no. 1, 2018, <www.assayjournal.com/philip-graham-the-shadow-knows-51.html>
2. Henry David Thoreau, *Familiar Letters: Volume VI*, Boston: Houghton, Mifflin and Co, 1906, Project Gutenberg, <www.gutenberg.org/cache/epub/43523/pg43523-images.html>
3. *Mr Fox* is an older version of the *Bluebeard* story recorded by Charles Perrault. *Mr Fox* was first recorded by John Blakeway in a 1790 edition of Shakespeare's plays. Shakespeare references 'the old tale' in his 1599 play *Much Ado About Nothing*, Act 1, scene 1, but it probably dates back hundreds of years before *Much Ado*. The version I have paraphrased (and quoted from) was recorded by Australian folklorist Joseph Jacobs in 1898. It can be found here: *English Fairy Tales* by Joseph Jacobs: 'Mr Fox', Authorama, December 2003, <www.authorama.com/english-fairy-tales-29.html>

Chapter 2 Back to the beginning

1. *This Changes Everything*, directed by Tom Donahue, CreativeChaos, 9 September 2018.
2. Robert W. Blum et al., 'It begins at 10: How gender expectations shape early adolescence around the world', *Journal of Adolescent Health*, vol. 61, issue 4, supp. S3–S4, 1 October 2017, DOI: <10.1016/j.jadohealth.2017.07.009>

Chapter 3 He's there again

1. Joseph Hurley, 'I Can't Believe I'm Still Protesting This Shit sign, Women's March on Washington, 2017-01-21', Georgia State University Library Exhibits, exhibits.library.gsu.edu/current/items/show/322.

Chapter 4 Trying to escape The Man
1. Gavin de Becker, *The Gift of Fear: Survival skills that protect us from violence*, London: Bloomsbury Publishing, 2000.
2. Maria Tumarkin, *Axiomatic*, Melbourne: Brow Books, 2018.
3. Kate Manne, *Down Girl: The logic of misogyny*, New York: Oxford University Press, 2017.
4. Melissa Davey, 'One in seven young Australians say rape justified if women change their mind, study finds', *The Guardian*, 22 May 2019, <www.theguardian.com/australia-news/2019/may/22/one-in-seven-young-australians-say-justified-if-women-change-their-mind-study-finds>
5. Editorial, 'The erosion of women's sexual and reproductive rights', *The Lancet*, vol. 393, 4 May 2019, <www.thelancet.com/action/showPdf?pii=S0140-6736%2819%2930990-0>

Chapter 6 Going to the police to report the stalking
1. Laura Richards, 'Domestic Abuse Bill New Clause 32 and 33: A legislative duty and national requirement to proactively identify, assess and manage serial and serious domestic violence perpetrators and stalkers', 5 July 2020, <www.laurarichards.co.uk/wp-content/uploads/2020/07/The-Domestic-Abuse-Bill-New-Clause-33-Serial-And-Serious-Domestic-Violence-Perpetrators-and-Stalkers-LCR-July-5-2020.pdf>
2. Shankar Vedantam (host), 'The Logic of Rage', *The Hidden Brain*, 6 October 2020, <https://hiddenbrain.org/podcast/the-logic-of-rage/>
3. Gavin de Becker, *The Gift of Fear*.
4. Soraya Chemaly, *Rage Becomes Her*, London: Simon & Schuster, 2018.
5. Shankar Vedantam, 'The Logic of Rage'.
6. Lilly Dancyger (ed.), *Burn It Down*, New York: Seal Press, 2019.
7. Samuel Brod et al., '"As above, so below" examining the interplay between emotion and the immune system', *Immunology*, vol. 143, no. 3, November 2014, DOI: <10.1111/imm.12341>

Chapter 7 Stalking and its toll on my mental health
1. 'Victim blaming', *The Why Factor*, BBC World Service, Radio, 6 January 2020.
2. Jane Gilmore, 'Fixed It because seriously, WTF', 10 July 2020, <janegilmore.com/fixed-it-because-seriously-wtf/>
3. Jane Gilmore, 'Fixed It: getting stabbed is not a "fight"', 9 July 2020, <janegilmore.com/fixed-it-getting-stabbed-is-not-a-fight/>

4. Jane Gilmore, 'Fixed It: what alleged crimes are you reporting?', 24 June 2020, <janegilmore.com/fixedit-what-alleged-crimes-are-you-reporting/>

Chapter 8 Women being silenced, a panic attack and a trip to Victim Support

1. Rebecca Solnit, 'Cassandra among the creeps', *Harper's Magazine*, October 2014, <https://harpers.org/archive/2014/10/cassandra-among-the-creeps/>
2. Lucia Osborne-Crowley, *I Choose Elena*, Crows Nest: Allen & Unwin, 2019.
3. Jackie Ashton, 'The art of saying no: how to raise kids to be polite, not pushovers', *The Washington Post,* 31 August 2019, <www.washingtonpost.com/lifestyle/on-parenting/the-art-of-saying-no-how-to-raise-kids-to-be-polite-not-pushovers/2016/08/30/9537e5d0-696c-11e6-ba32-5a4bf5aad4fa_story.html>
4. Sri Wahyuningsih, 'Men and women differences in using language: a case study of students at STAIN Kudus', *EduLite Journal of English Education, Literature and Culture*, vol. 3, no. 1, February 2018, DOI: <10.30659/e.3.1.79-90>
5. Nina Eliasoph, 'Politeness, power and women's language: rethinking study in language and gender', *Berkeley Journal of Sociology,* vol. 32, pp. 79–103, <www.jstor.org/stable/41035360?origin=JSTOR-pdf&seq=1>

Chapter 9 Has The Man been to my house?

1. Amanda Hooton, 'Sixth sense: the science behind intuition', *The Sydney Morning Herald*, 24 April 2021, <www.smh.com.au/lifestyle/life-and-relationships/sixth-sense-the-science-behind-intuition-20210304-p577wm.html>
2. Duncan Banks, 'What is brain plasticity and why is it so important?', *The Conversation*, 5 April 2016, <https://theconversation.com/what-is-brain-plasticity-and-why-is-it-so-important-55967>
3. Judith Herman, *Trauma and Recovery*, New York: Basic Books, 1992.
4. Bessel van der Kolk, *The Body Keeps the Score*, UK: Penguin, 2014.
5. Deborah Epstein and Lisa Goodman, *Discounting Women: Doubting domestic violence survivors' credibility and dismissing their experiences*, Washington: Georgetown University Law Centre, 2019, <https://scholarship.law.georgetown.edu/cgi/viewcontent.cgi?article=3055&context=facpub>
6. Gavin de Becker, *The Gift of Fear.*

7. Mark Evans et al., *From Girls to Men: Social attitudes to gender equality in Australia*, 50/50 Foundation, 2018, <www.5050 foundation.edu.au/assets/reports/documents/From-Girls-to-Men.pdf>

8. Stephanie Richards, 'Harassment inquiry into SA legal profession "unnecessary": Law Society', *InDaily*, 19 October 2020, <https://indaily.com.au/news/2020/10/19/harassment-inquiry-into-sa-legal-profession-unnecessary-law-society/>

9. 'Donald Trump says sexual assault accuser E Jean Carroll "not my type"', *The Guardian Australia*, 25 June 2019, <www.theguardian.com/us-news/2019/jun/25/donald-trump-says-assault-accuser-e-jean-carroll-not-my-type>

10. Mark Makela, 'Transcript: Donald Trump's taped comments about women', *The New York Times*, 8 October 2016, <www.nytimes.com/2016/10/08/us/donald-trump-tape-transcript.html>
Incidentally, when I viewed this page in *The New York Times*, a clickbait advert popped up among the text. It was a photograph of Pauley Perrette (Abby in NCIS) with the caption 'Remember her? Take a deep breath before you see what she looks like now'. The 'article' it led to was entitled '42 stars who have aged, but still look flawlessly amazing', with accompanying 'then and now' photos so you could compare the younger versions with the older. Every single one of them was a woman. A reminder that it's not just Donald Trump and Billy Bush that view women as objects to be looked at, prized first and foremost for their beauty.

Chapter 10 The search for security

1. Kathryn Hughes, 'Gender roles in the 19th century', *Discovering Literature: Romantics and Victorians*, British Library, 15 May 2014, <www.bl.uk/romantics-and-victorians/articles/gender-roles-in-the-19th-century>

2. Anne Stiles, 'Go rest, young man', *American Psychological Association*, vol. 43, no. 1, January 2012, <www.apa.org/monitor/2012/01/go-rest>

3. Charlotte P. Stetson, 'The yellow wallpaper: a story', *The New England Magazine*, vol. 11, no. 5, January 1892, pp. 647–56.

4. Married Jake, 'Why men love to take care of you', *Glamour*, 13 April 2009, <www.glamour.com/story/why-men-love-to-take-care-of-you>

Chapter 11 Things I do to stay sane

1. Erica Hornstein and Naomi Eisenberger, 'Unpacking the buffering effect of social support figures: social support attenuates fear

acquisition', *PLOS ONE*, vol. 12, no. 5, May 2017, DOI: <10.1371/journal.pone.0175891>

Chapter 12 The Man sends me a Facebook message
1. Brian H. Spitzberg and William R. Cupach, 'The state of the art of stalking: taking stock of the emerging literature', *Aggression and Violent Behaviour 12*, February 2007, pp. 64–86.

Chapter 13 Confronting The Man
1. 'Victim Blaming', *The Why Factor*.
2. World Health Organization, 'Violence against women', World Health Organization Fact Sheets, 29 November 2017, <www.who.int/news-room/fact-sheets/detail/violence-against-women>
3. Sherry Hamby, *Battered Women's Protective Strategies: Stronger than you know*, New York: Oxford University Press, 2013, <www.freestatesocialwork.com/articles/AR_BWProtStrat.pdf>

Chapter 14 The Man appears in my local café
1. Galina Daraganova, '6. Self-harm and suicidal behaviour of young people aged 14–15 years old', in The Longitudinal Study of Australian Children, *Annual Statistical Report 2016*, Australian Institute of Family Studies, August 2017, <www.growingupinaustralia.gov.au/research-findings/annual-statistical-report-2016/self-harm-and-suicidal-behaviour-young-people-aged-14-15-years-old>
2. Ellie Mae O'Hagan, 'Women's self-harm is being fuelled by misogyny', *The Guardian Australia*, 29 August 2018, <www.theguardian.com/commentisfree/2018/aug/29/women-self-harm-misogyny-social-pressure-pain>
3. Bessel van der Kolk, *The Body Keeps the Score*.
4. Galina Daragovna, '6. Self-harm and suicidal behaviour of young people aged 14–15 years old'.

Chapter 15 An overseas reprieve
1. *Unfollow Me*, Vice Media Group, 2018, <www.vice.com/en/topic/unfollow-me>
2. Legal Services Commission of South Australia, *Legal Help for All South Australians: Stalking*, 2018, <lawhandbook.sa.gov.au/ch21s07s05s03.php>
3. Victoria University, *Stalking*, 2020, <www.vu.edu.au/about-vu/facilities-services/safer-community/concerning-threatening-or-inappropriate-behaviour/stalking>
4. Emma Ogilvie, *Stalking: policing and prosecuting practices in three Australian jurisdictions*, Australian Institute of Criminology, 2000, <www.aic.gov.au/sites/default/files/2020-05/tandi176.pdf>

5. All statistics retrieved from: UN Women, 'Facts and figures: ending violence against women', updated November 2020, <www.unwomen.org/en/what-we-do/ending-violence-against-women/facts-and-figures>

Chapter 16 Resurgence of fear

1. Rachel Mackenzie et al., 'Types of stalking', *Stalking Risk Profile*, StalkInc., 2011, <www.stalkingriskprofile.com/what-is-stalking/types-of-stalking>
2. Ginger Gorman, *Troll Hunting*, Melbourne: Hardie Grant, 2019.
3. Robyn M. Dawes, 'A message from psychologists to economists: mere predictability doesn't matter like it should (without a good story appended to it)', *Science Direct*, vol. 39, no. 1, May 1999, <doi.org/10.1016/S0167-2681(99)00024-4>
4. Shelley C. Spiecker and Debra L. Worthington, 'The influence of opening statement/closing argument organizational strategy on juror verdict and damage awards 1', *Law and Human Behaviour*, vol. 7, no. 4, September 2003, pp. 438–9, DOI: <10.1023/A:1024041201605>
5. Shankar Vedantam (host), 'The story of stories', *The Hidden Brain*, 16 March 2021, <https://hiddenbrain.org/podcast/the-story-of-stories/>
6. William R. Bascom, 'Four functions of folklore', *The Journal of American Folklore*, vol. 67, no. 266, pp. 333–49, October–December 1954, <doi.org/10.2307/536411>
7. W.E.B. Du Bois, 'Criteria of Negro Art', *The Crisis*, vol. 32, pp. 290–7, Oct 1926.
8. Jess Hill, *See What You Made Me Do*, Melbourne: Black Inc., 2019.

Chapter 17 Why is misogyny so persistent?

1. Shankar Vedantam (host), 'Radically normal', *The Hidden Brain*, 9 March 2021, <https://hiddenbrain.org/podcast/radically-normal/>
2. Saadia Zahidi, 'Accelerating gender parity in Globalization 4.0', World Economic Forum, 18 June 2019, <https://www.weforum.org/agenda/2019/06/accelerating-gender-gap-parity-equality-globalization-4/>
3. Allan G. Johnson, *The Gender Knot: Unraveling our patriarchal legacy*, 3rd ed., Philadelphia: Temple University Press, 2014.
4. Blair Williams, '"Expect sexism": a gender politics expert reads Julia Gillard's Women and Leadership', *The Conversation*, 17 July 2020, <https://theconversation.com/expect-sexism-a-gender-politics-expert-reads-julia-gillards-women-and-leadership-142725>

5. Kate Manne, *Entitled: How male privilege hurts women*, UK: Penguin Books, 2021.
6. Jess Hill, *See What You Made Me Do*.
7. Gus Worland (creator), *Man Up*, Series 1, Episodes 1–3, ABC, 2016, <www.iview.abc.net.au/video/DO1504H001S00>
8. Nina Eliasoph, 'Politeness, power and women's language'.
9. Malcolm Gladwell, *Blink: The power of thinking without thinking*, UK: Penguin Books, 2006.
10. Gavin de Becker, *The Gift of Fear*.

Chapter 18 Changing our thinking

1. Peter Adams, 'Nando's tackled the inauguration with a bold campaign—and saw a 122% sales lift', Marketing Dive, 24 May 2017, <https://www.marketingdive.com/news/nandos-tackled-the-inauguration-with-a-bold-campaign-and-saw-a-122-sale/443368/>
2. Guardian News, 'Kamala Harris's historic victory speech in full: "You chose truth"', YouTube, 7 November 2020, <www.youtube.com/watch?v=MXnePLTILY4>
3. Guardian News, 'Joe Biden's victory speech in full: "We must restore the soul of America"', YouTube, 7 November 2020, <www.youtube.com/watch?v=yX20JkK5L3s>
4. Ian Leslie, *Conflicted: Why arguments are tearing us apart and how they can bring us back together*, London: Faber, 2021.
5. Ginger Gorman, *Troll Hunting*.
6. Nisha Anand, 'The radical act of choosing common ground', TED Talks, 16 March 2020, <www.ted.com/talks/nisha_anand_the_radical_act_of_choosing_common_ground_nov_2020?language=en>
7. Howard Rheingold, 'The new power of collaboration', TED Talks, February 2005, <www.ted.com/talks/howard_rheingold_the_new_power_of_collaboration#t-1439>
8. Phumzile Mlambo-Ngcuka, 'Statement by Phumzile Mlambo-Ngcuka, UN Women Executive Director, on the International Day for the Elimination of Violence against Women', UN Women, 25 November 2020, <www.unwomen.org/en/news/stories/2020/11/statement-ed-phumzile-international-day-for-the-elimination-of-violence-against-women>
9. UN Women, 'Infographic: The shadow pandemic—violence against women and girls and COVID-19', 6 April 2020, <www.unwomen.org/en/digital-library/multimedia/2020/4/infographic-covid19-violence-against-women-and-girls>
10. Male Champions of Change, 'Male Champions of Change—Our journey', 22 November 2017, <https://championsofchangecoalition.org/our-journey/>

11. 'Sex discrimination, sexual harassment and predatory behaviour in South Australia Police', South Australian Equal Opportunities Commission, Adelaide, November 2016, <https://www.eoc.sa.gov.au/documents/SAPOL_Review_2016_Final.pdf>

12. David Rutledge (host), 'Structural injustice and individual responsibility', *The Philosopher's Zone*, ABC Radio National, 2 January 2022, www.abc.net.au/radionational/programs/philosopherszone/structural-injustice-and-individual-responsibility/13486680

13. David Olds, Peggy Hill and Elissa Rumsey, 'Prenatal and early childhood nurse home visitation', *Juvenile Justice Bulletin*, Office of Juvenile Justice and Deliquency Prevention, US Department of Justice, November 1998, <www.ojp.gov/pdffiles/172875.pdf>

14. David Olds, Lisa M. Pettitt et al., 'Reducing risks for antisocial behavior with a program of prenatal and early childhood home visitation', *Journal of Community Psychology*, vol. 26, no. 1, 1998, pp. 65–83, DOI: <10.1002/(SICI)1520-6629(199801)26:1<65::AID-JCOP6>3.0.CO;2-0>

15. David Olds, John Eckenrode et al., 'Long-term effects of home visitation on maternal life course and child abuse and neglect: 15-year follow-up of a randomized trial', *Journal of the Medical Association*, vol. 278, no. 8, August 1997, pp. 637–43, DOI: <10.1001/jama.1997.03550080047038>

16. David Olds, Charles R. Henderson Jr, Robert Chamberlin and Robert Tatelbaum, 'Preventing child abuse and neglect: a randomized trial of nurse home visitation', *Pediatrics*, vol. 78, no. 1, 1986, pp. 65–78, <https://doi.org/10.1542/peds.78.1.65>

17. David Olds, Charles R. Henderson Jr et al., 'Long-term effects of nurse home visitation on children's criminal and antisocial behavior: 15-year follow-up of a randomized controlled trial', *Journal of the Medical Association*, vol. 280, no. 14, 1998, pp. 1238–44, DOI: <10.1001/jama.280.14.1238>

18. David Olds, Charles R. Henderson Jr et al., 'Long-term effects of nurse home visitation on children's criminal and antisocial behavior'.

19. Daily Wire, 'Shapiro wrecks Nike's new "bold" ad', The Ben Shapiro Show, Episode 724, YouTube, 26 February 2019, <www.youtube.com/watch?v=RN0e_TZCXl0>